RHYME'S RE

THIRD EDITION

JOHN HOLLANDER

Rhyme's Reason

A GUIDE TO ENGLISH VERSE

NB YALE NOTA BENE

Yale University Press

New Haven & London

For information about this and other Yale University Press
publications, please contact:
U.S. office   sales.press@yale.edu
Europe office   sales@yaleup.co.uk

Printed in the United States of America.

Library of Congress catalog card number: 00-043375
ISBN 0-300-08832-9 (pbk.)

A catalog record for this book is available from the British
Library.

10   9   8   7   6   5   4

For Lizzy and Martha

Chosen illustrations of form get dafter
As they shy from *Familiar Quotations;*
Most examples follow too slowly after
          Their explanations,

Though even if I could improve the timing
There's no one I could trust to do the graphics
And so, even as now I do in rhyming
          Horace's sapphics,

Scorning such an account of rhyme as uses
Assembly-line quotations, then, I fill a
Book with verses handmade, the sterner Muses'
          Laughing ancilla.

CONTENTS

PREFACE TO THE
THIRD EDITION

In the second edition of this hand-book, I added a considerable bit of new material; this included some non-Western verse forms influential to poets writing in English; a discussion of what the late W. K. Wimsatt called "verbal mimesis"; and some examples, self-descriptive in various ways—such as sonnets on the sonnet—of verse forms by other poets from the seventeenth through the twentieth centuries. This considerably augmented third edition allows the schemes and patterns illustrated self-descriptively additional room to speak for themselves, as it were, through instances of their actual use in poetry. These are collected in the section Patterns in Practice at the end of this volume and will additionally exemplify the ways in which different historical styles of diction and syntax, and changing conceptions of genre, have subtly recast older formal patterns and devices.

I should like to head off any possible misleading characterization of this book as a guide to "formal poetry." The very term itself seems a misnomer: it implies that accentual-syllabic verse is the only "form," and that the many different kinds of free-verse, of twentieth-century syllabics, of pure accentualism, etc., are formless. This is nonsense. There is a great difference between coherent writing and incoherent or dysfunctional writing in verse of any sort. And surely poetic "form" is a very deep matter that covers much more than phonological or typographic pattern. I have discussed such matters in some detail elsewhere; but a reader who considers closely the array of examples now included will probably be able to see into some of these depths.

Since the original edition of this manual twenty years ago, I have noticed that a considerable number of good younger poets are now writing accentual-syllabic (rhymed or blank) or syllabic verse with deep skill, or various modes of free verse that generate their own conventions and rules with the same kind of power that measured verse deploys. This is perhaps because a century-long tradition of great poetry written in free verse can supply models, not for imitation, but—and this is true of all poetic verbal patterns—for creative revision. And yet the preponderance of very bad verse is still the same weak *vers libre* that has all of the inanity of the rhymed greeting-card jingle that was the analogous default-mode of badly written verse in the first half of the twentieth century. Good verse of any sort is nevertheless only half the story of good poetry, whose essential character is what Wallace Stevens called "fictive," and Robert Frost "ulterior," or "saying one thing and meaning another," or what we could simply call not being literal. Having in the past year spent time recovering from an injury, I came to realize that "When you see someone with a cane / That person's probably in pain."

These lines are clearly verse, and the proposition they assert is true. But they are not in the least *poetry*, for they are totally literal: there is nothing of fiction in them. Even the one possible trace of the nonliteral that might lurk therein—that *pain* and *cane* appropriately rhyme because feeling the first might lead one to use the second—is totally glossed into triviality by the simple literal truth of the statement. *Rhyme's Reason* is thus subtitled *A Guide to English Verse* and not "—*to Poetry*." I trust that its readers will understand that verse (or in certain modern instances, prose treated and used as verse) is a necessary but not a sufficient condition for poetry. All the rest is metaphor.

I hope that immediate reminders of the actual poetic use of the patterns and schemes will inform readers' subsequent experience of the whole of poetry in our language.

I have corrected a few minor errors and added to the main body of the text some material on conventions of typographical indentation in verse. In addition I should like to add the following to the "Suggestions for Further Reading" section on page 137–138: Paul Fry's *The Poet's Calling in the English Ode* (New Haven, 1980); Jennifer Wagner's *Moment's Monument: Revisionary Poetics and the Nineteenth-Century Sonnet* (Madison, N.J., 1996); John Fuller's *The Sonnet* (London, 1972); Stephen Cushman's *Fictions of Form in Modern Poetry* (Princeton, 1993); Richard Bradford's *The Look of It: A Theory of Visual Form in English Poetry* (Cork, Ireland, 1993); Annie Finch's *The Ghost of Meter: Culture and Prosody in American Free Verse* (Ann Arbor, 1993); H. T. Kirby-Smith's *The Origins of Free Verse* (Ann Arbor, 1996); and Steven Monte's *Invisible Fences: Prose Poetry as a Genre in French and American Literature* (Lincoln, Nebr., 2000).

I wish to thank Donald Hall and Alan Ansen for permission to include their splendidly self-regarding sestinas.

his is a guide to verse, to the formal structures which are a necessary condition of poetry, but not a sufficient one. The building blocks of poetry itself are elements of fiction—fable, "image," metaphor—all the material of the nonliteral. The components of verse are like parts of plans by which the materials are built into a structure. The study of rhetoric distinguishes between tropes, or figures of meaning such as metaphor and metonymy, and schemes, or surface patterns of words. Poetry is a matter of trope; and verse, of scheme or design. But the blueprints of verse can be used to build things made of literal, or nonpoetic material—a shopping list or roadside sign can be rhymed—which is why most verse is not poetry.

It is nonetheless common and convenient for most people who don't read carefully to use "poetry" to mean "writing in some kind of verse," and to regard thereby the design without considering the materials. The most popular verse form in America today—the ubiquitous jingle readers identify with "poetry" even as, fifty or sixty years ago, they did anything that rhymed—is

a kind of free verse
without any special
constraints on it except
those imposed by
the notion—also
generally accepted—that
the strip the lines
make as they run
down the page (the
familiar strip with the
jagged
right-hand edge) not
be too wide

This is as automatic and unpoetic in its arbitrary formality as jingling rhymes on "June" and "moon" ever were; schemes and structures of free verse are as conventional and, for most writers, as "academic" as certain other "official" forms have been in other eras. Major poetry has been built in this form, even as Tennyson could employ the same rhyming schemes as writers of occasional verses for family parties.

Both verse and prose, then, are schematic domains. Literacy used to entail some ability to write in both modes, without any presumption of poetry in the execution of skill in the former. But today sportswriters on the few newspapers we have left know no Latin nor can write good witty verses. We no longer memorize poems at school. Young persons are protected from the prose cadences—so influential on writing in both modes—of the King James Bible by aggressive separatism and the churches themselves; all of us are shielded from Shakespearean rhythm by the ways in which both prose and verse are publicly intoned in America. The territory covered in this guide—this road map through the region of poetry in English—has itself tended to run back into second-growth timber, if not into wilderness.

Some day we will all be reading Blue Guides and Baedekers to what once were our own, familiar public places. In former times, the region of verse was like an inviting, safe municipal park, in which one could play and wander at will. Today, only a narrow border of that park is frequently used (and vandalized), out of fear that there is safety only in that crowded strip— even as the users' grandparents would cling to walks

that went by statues—and out of ignorance of land-
scape. The beauties of the rest of that park are there,
unexplored save by some scholars and often aban-
doned even by them.

I am old enough to have grown up in the park,
and to map a region one loves is a way of caressing
it. (Goethe wrote of counting out hexameters on his
Roman lady's back as she lay in his arms: he was
mapping her body's curve even as he felt for the
ancient rhythm.) I too set out now as a loving rather
than merely dutiful tour guide. Even today, when
touch seems casual and only discourse intimate, one
can't presume on Whitmanic relations with readers.
I shall content myself (Inquiry's too severe in prose; /
Verse puts its questions in repose) with tapping out
my self-explaining diagrams and illustrations of the
walks and alleys and bosks and ponds and parterres
and follies and hahas and so forth that comprise my
territory, as it were, on the reader's hand. After all,
this *is* a manual.

The schemes and designs to be explored here include: the structures of lines of verse; patterns of
rhyme, alliteration, and assonance; schemes of syntax and word order; groups of lines called strophes
or stanzas; overall patterns of repetition and variation
(refrains, etc.); and larger arrangements of these.
Over the centuries, these forms have come at various
times to be associated with one or another kind of
poetic use—or with what some critics would call a
"theme," a "subject" or an occasion. Sonnets, for
example, start out by being about a particular philosophic conception of love, and end up in the twen-

tieth century as descriptions of pictures, explanations of myths, or analytic meditations. And yet the later poems in the history of the form's life—when written by the finest poets—are always in some way aware of, and always engage, that history and the burden it puts on originality.

This little book contains examples of formal schemes of various sorts, and at various levels of organization. Since we are concerned only with verse in English, no historical sketch or comparative analysis of metrics and forms is given, save for a glance at what the meters of classical poetry have entailed for English. But it should be remembered that all poetry was originally oral. It was sung or chanted; poetic scheme and musical pattern coincided, or were sometimes identical. Poetic form as we know it is an abstraction from, or residue of, musical form, from which it came to be divorced when writing replaced memory as a way of preserving poetic utterance in narrative, prayer, spell, and the like. The ghost of oral poetry never vanishes, even though the conventions and patterns of writing reach out across time and silence all actual voices. This is why, to go back to the earlier analogy of architecture, a poet is always like both the builder of houses, with plans "at hand," and the designer or executor of a complicated edifice, drawing and working from complex blueprints.

Verse can be organized according to very many metrical *systems*, depending upon the structure of the language in which the verse is written. The systems relevant to verse in English are:

1. *Pure accentual*—the meter of the earliest Ger-

manic poetry; it is preserved in nursery rhymes and in much lyric verse.

2. *Accentual-syllabic*—the verse system which involves such patterns as "iambic," "dactylic," etc., all somewhat confusingly named for Greek meters in a totally different system.

3. *Pure syllabic*—the basic system of modern French and Japanese, to cite two kinds of poetry that have used it for centuries; it has been used in English only in the last fifty years or so.

4. So-called *free verse*, of which there are many varieties, developed mostly in the twentieth century.

5. *Quantitative verse* which, save for some grotesque and failed examples, cannot occur in English, but which was the basis of Greek prosody and, later on, of Latin.

Since accentual-syllabism has been so dominant, and so important, during the course of the poetic history of the English language, we will start with it.

Accentual-syllabic verse is built up of pairs or triads of syllables, alternating or otherwise grouping stressed and unstressed ones. Syllables usually keep their word accent, or the accent they would have in phrases in normal speech. *Iambic pentameter*, a line pattern made up of five syllable pairs with the first syllable unstressed, can be illustrated by a line which most perfectly conforms to the pattern itself:

About about about about about

or this:

A boat, a boat, a boat, a boat, a boat

(for a monosyllable, with its preceding article, is accented like a word of two syllables). But actual lines of iambic pentameter, because they can't simply repeat identical pairs of syllables, have individual and particular rhythms which depart from the metrical pattern slightly. It is in this variation that the sound of poetry lives. For example, a simple variation of our first example—one that has become a standard pattern in itself—is actually a reversal of stressed and unstressed syllables in the first pair:

> *Al*most *"about about about about"*

or in the second as well:

> *Nearly al*most *"about about about"*

But there are ways of departing that seem to obscure the pattern so that they can no longer be considered variations from it:

> *Al*most the *sound* of the *line* of *"about"*s

What we hear is a rhythm of four beats, not five, and the unstressed syllables are grouped into triads of *dum* de de, *dum* de de (called dactyls), even though there are, in fact, ten syllables in the lines.

Most interesting with regard to poetry are the variations—and almost every line of poetry exhibits them—that lie between these extremes. Any poem will be cast in one metrical form or another, and after we read three or more lines it will be obvious which of two patterns even the most ambiguous line is a variation of. Frequently, richness and significance of sound depend upon our ear hesitating for a while between patterns; but there is real ambiguity only

at the start of a poem. An extreme case is the opening
of one of Keats's sonnets:

How many bards gild the lapses of time

We might think that a matching line would be:

Read this as dactyls and then it will rhyme

like the one we made up before. But in fact, the
sonnet continues in iambic pentameter, and we realize that we had a wildly variant first line instead
of a more patterned one. But a better example, also
by Keats, can be seen in the second line of his "Ode
on a Grecian Urn":

Thou fóster-chíld of sílence and slów tíme

Here, although only the fourth pair has its order
reversed, the line nevertheless resounds with other
possibilities. Thus,

Thou fóster-child of sílence and slów tíme
Accéntually poúnding to só míme
An antiquated rhýthm which had nó rhýme.

But the phrase "slow time" resolves itself in the poem
because "time" rhymes there only with the monosyllable "rhyme" two lines below (there's no "slow"/
"so" chiming, as in our example). When we *scan* a
line of poetry, or mark the prominent syllables, we
are really showing what its actual rhythm is, and
then, by putting this rhythm in alignment with adjacent ones in the poem or stanza of the poem, de-
ciding what their common pattern is. Thus, every
line is at once unique and has family resemblances,
usually very strong, to its companions in any one
poem.

Accentual-syllabic verse is traditionally discussed
as sequences of *feet*; and although the terminology
is misleading, you can remember that:

A foót | is júst | a groúp | of sýl- | lablés:
Tróchees | (like these), | iámbs, | spóndees, | paíred, while
Dactyls and | anapests | álways are | triads of | sýllables.

An iamb is a pair with a stress on the second syllable
(as in "about"):

Iámbic méter rúns alóng like thís:
Pentameters will have five syllables
More strongly stressed than other ones nearby—
Ten syllables all told, perhaps eleven.

But

Tróchees símply túmble oń and
Start with downbeats just like this one
(Sorry, "iamb" is trochaic).

★

"Dactyl" means | "fínger" in | Gréek, and a | foót that was
| máde up of | ońe lońg
Syllable followed by two, like the joints in a finger was used
for
Lines made of six, just like these, in the epics of Homer and
Virgil,
Save that in English we substitute downbeats and upbeats
for long-short.*

★

In an *ań | apest* up | beats start oút | in revérse
Of the dactyl's persuasion but end up no worse.
(Yes, the anapest's name is dactylic—a curse?)

★

Slow *spóndees* are two héavy stressed dównbeats
They stand shoulder to strong shoulder this way.

*For more on this, see pages 34–36.

We can even observe the echoes of such accentual "feet" in natural speech:

> Só names such as "Jóhn Smíth" seém spóndees.
> (Names of pláces, such as "Maín Street"?*
> Thése are mérely goód old tróchees.)

It will be clear by now that different kinds of accentual-syllabic line will "interpret" a stress-pattern of natural speech in different ways. Disyllabic words are stressed either one way or another, and pairs of words that differ by virtue of stress alone will have to play different metrical roles:

> These línes can shów you whére the accént wént,
> Bút with their cóntent I'm not yét contént.

And trisyllables, for example, can submit to two readings. We would say that "typewriter" is normally dactyllic-sounding, and placing it in a dactyllic line elicits this character.

> Lísten, my týpewriter clátters in dáctyls alóng with my
>   próse!

But "typewriter" is a compound word, once hyphenated ("type-writer") before constant use in speech had silenced the second stress; that ghost of accent can be summoned up:

> My týpewríter in vérse divídes its tíme
> Between iamb and trochee. (Now I'll rhyme.)

Clearly, a little phrase like "open it" will work like a dactyllic single word, just as "of the best" will work like an anapestic one. It will be apparent, also, that accentual-syllabic verse can make much of the variations of stress that occur when we are logically con-

---

*(But a tówn's "maín streét" 's spondáic.)

trasting two words or phrases which differ by reason
of their unstressed syllable. "A book" is an iamb; so
is "the book"; but what we write as "*the* book" (and
pronounce as something like "thee book") promotes
the unstressed syllable, in emphatic contrast, to
something having more of the power of "this book"
or "that book." Thus we might, iambically,

> Observe the whore outside the store.

But if we mean to single out the allegorical figure of
Revelation 17 then she may become trochaic, when

> Bábylón we meán here—*the* whore
> (Not some hooker by the seashore):

When the older terminology of "foot" for "syllable
pair" or "triad" is used, line length is described in
terms of number of feet, as for example *di*meter,
*tri*meter:

> If she should write
> Some verse tonight
> This dimeter
> Would limit her.

But:

> Iambic trimeter
> Is rather easier.

And:

> Tetrámeter allows more space
> For thoughts to seat themselves with grace.

Now:

> Here is *pentámeter*, the line of five
> That English poetry still keeps alive;

In other centuries it was official.
Now, different kinds of verse make it seem special.

★

Six downbeats in a line that has twelve syllables
Make up the *alexandrine*, which, as you can hear,
Tends to fall into halves—one question, one reply.

The break that you heard in the last line is called
caesura. Here it is at work in rhymed pairs of lines
called *couplets:*

In couplets, one line often makes a point
Which hinges on its bending, like a joint;
The sentence makes that line break into two.
Here's a *caesura:* see what it can do.
(And here's a gentler one, whose pause, more slight,
Waves its two hands, and makes what's left sound right.)

Two even longer measured lines:

Fourteeners, cut from *ballad stanzas*, don't seem right for song:
Their measure rumbles on like this for just a bit too long.

and, used by early Elizabethans,

A *poulter's measure* (like a baker's dozen) cut
One foot off a fourteener couplet, ended in a rut.

Let us now consider groupings of lines, by rhyme
or other means, remembering first that

A line can be *end-stopped*, just like this one,
Or it can show *enjambment*, just like this
One, where the sense straddles two lines: you feel
As if from shore you'd stepped into a boat;

and remembering secondly that there is a unique
case, outside of line-groups. The one-line poem (in
Greek, a *monostich*) is almost always really a couplet,

an epigram formed by the title and the line itself, as in

A ONE-LINE POEM

The universe

First, then, *blank verse:*

Iambic five-beat lines are labeled *blank*
Verse (with sometimes a foot or two reversed,
Or one more syllable—"feminine ending").
Blank verse can be extremely flexible:
It ticks and tocks the time with even feet
(Or sometimes, cleverly, can end limping).*
Shakespeare and others of his day explored
Blank verse in stage plays, both in regular
And rather uneven and more rough-hewn forms.
Occasionally, rhyming couplets sound
Out at scenes' endings, gongs to end the round.
Milton did other things: he made it more
Heroic than dramatic: although blind
He turned its structure into something half
Heard, half seen, as when a *chiasm*†
(Words, phrases, sounds or parts of speech arranged
In mirroring) occurs in *Paradise*
Lost (he often *enjambs* this way) we see
Half a line that, reflecting its line-half,
Cannot sit still to be regarded like
A well-made picture or inscription, but
Rushes ahead as sentences do, not like
Visual melody in a well-shaped line.
But back again to what blank verse can do:
In time of old, inversions it contained
Of syntax, and Wordsworth and Tennyson
More delicately such arrangements made.
But Browning and more lately Robert Frost
Made their blank verse seem natural again,
The kind of sound our sentences would make

*(Pentameters like this are called *scazons*.)
†And see page 49.

If only we could leave them to themselves—
The road our way of talking always takes,
Not, like a foul line or state boundary,
An artificially drawn line at all.

But:

The old fourteener William Blake found to his liking more
Than old "heroic" verse, pentameters, which must have
    seemed
Far too *official* for him; so, like Milton with his ten
Syllables, Blake pushed ahead with the seven stresses he
    heard beneath
The even fourteeners sanctified for him by balladry
(For two rhyming fourteeners can / be written out, you see,
In just a single ballad stan- / za, rhymed *abab*)
And common hymnody, and Chapman's *Iliad*, and all
Popular rhyming forms eschewed by Alexander Pope.
Blake, in *Jerusalem* and *Milton*, twisted the seven-beat line
With terrible vatic force, & claimed that he wrote in three
    different keys,
"Terrific," "Mild & gentle," and "Prosaic"; yet it remains
Hard to distinguish their tones, as it were, from rhythmic
    patterns alone.

Before we move into groupings made by rhyme,
let us consider the ways in which syllables themselves can reach through, or across, lines. They can
alliterate:

Alliteration lightly links
Stressed syllables with common consonants.

And they can, without actually rhyming, exhibit
assonance:

Assonance is the spirit of a rhyme,
A common vowel, hovering like a sigh
After its consonantal body dies.

We should also remember the following, about rhyme
itself:

The weakest way in which two words can chime
Is with the most expected kind of rhyme—
(If it's the only rhyme that you can write,
A homophone will never sound quite right.)
A rhyme is stronger when the final words
Seem less alike than pairs of mated birds.
When meaning makes a gap which sound can span, it's
As if the rhyme words came from different planets;
Or when a final verb, perhaps, will reach
Out to rhyme with some different part of speech;
Or when a word spelled in one way, like "off,"
Rhymes strictly, with a sort of visual cough
Of surprise; or when a common word like "love"
Which rhymed in Shakespeare's time with "move" and
    "prove"
Ends up today a sight-rhyme, as above.
Some rhymes can trip you as you move along:
Their lines can seem as smooth as they are strong.
Like a typewriter's final, right-hand bell,
A rhyme can stop a line, or it can tell
The sentence to go on and do its best
Till, at the next line's end, it comes to rest.
And if the tone shows signs of letting up, let
There be a cute rhyme for a final couplet.
(A serious effect is often killable
By rhyming with *too* much more than one syllable.)

Internal rhymes can claim a word or name
And make two words mean something of the same:
Thus *spring* can *jingle* with its *singing* birds,
Or *summer hum* with two resounding words;
The red *robes* of *October's* garish ball
Make *fall recall* that dropping leaves are all
We hear; the hard, dry stint of winter lasts
Through blizzards and through *slow* and *snowy* blasts,
Until lengthening sunlight hours will bring
Round in a *ring*like way again, the *spring*.

One of the most important groupings of lines we
have had in English, particularly in the seventeenth
through the nineteenth centuries, has been the English couplet, paired rhymed iambic pentameter:

Heroic couplets, classical and cold,
Can make new matters smack of something old
And something borrowed (like a wedding, true,
But this comparison stops short of "blue"
Yet points out how the marriage of two lines ⎫
Brings forth long children as their length combines ⎬
—And sometimes triplets help to vary the designs). ⎭
This verse was called "heroic" for the way
It seemed equivalent, in Jonson's day—
The seventeenth century—to Homer's long
Unrhymed hexameters, and Virgil's song.
With Alexander Pope, we have so pure a
Way of arranging these, that a *caesura*
Makes this line pause, makes that one slowly wend
Its way to join its partner in the end.
An *end-stopped* line is one—as you'll have guessed—
Whose syntax comes, just at its end, to rest.
But when the walking sentence needs to keep
On going, the *enjambment* makes a leap
Across a line-end (here, a rhyming close).
—Milton, in his blank verse, makes use of those:
His long, dependent clauses are enjambed.
A somewhat sharp effect, as well, is damned
Easy—when, reading on, the reader learns
The maze of verse can have its sudden turns
And twists—but couplets take your hand, and then
Lead you back into end-stopped rhyme again.

Of course,

Couplets can be of any length,
And shorter size gives greater strength
Sometimes—but sometimes, willy-nilly,
Four-beat couplets sound quite silly.
(Some lines really should stay single:
Feminine rhymes can make them jingle.)

These *anapestic tetrameter* couplets, by the way,
were used widely in the late eighteenth and the early
nineteenth centuries; they can seem either active or
passively elegiac:

There are rhythms like this that you'll frequently meet:
They resound with the pounding of regular feet,
And their anapests carry a narrative load
(The hoofbeats of horses, of course, on the road).

★

But they lie by the side of a whispering stream
Flowing slowly as time, gliding by in a dream.

Now, then:

Tercets are groups of three; they are a band
—Playful, like couplets that get out of hand—
Of lines that fly far, then come back to land.

★

A *quatrain* has four lines
    As one can plainly see:
One of its strict designs
    Comes rhymed *abab*.

★

Another way of rhyme can come
    From *abba* (middle two
    Lines holding hands as lovers do)
In Tennyson's *In Memoriam*.

★

After the heyday of such rhyme's renown,
After the weariness of World War I,
Modern poets built in a sad letdown
By rhyming quatrains thus: *abax*.

★

The *ballad stanza*'s four short lines
    Are very often heard;
The second and the fourth lines rhyme
    But not the first and third.

★

The ballad stanza in a hymn
    Waits on the music's pleasure,

And hymnals (hardly out of whim)
  Call it the "common measure."

★

(The attic heart's—theology
Reformed—this hymnal scheme
In Emily Dickinson's—Amherst—house
And slanted—away—the rhyme.)

★

"Long measure" in the hymnody
Means even quatrains just like this,
Whose music sets the spirit free,
Doctrine dissolved in choral bliss.

★

Translating Omar Khayyam's *Rubaiyat*,
Edward Fitzgerald, it would seem, forgot
   To rhyme the third line with the other ones.
(The last line underscored its lonely lot.)

He didn't, really: I meant no aspersion.
His gloomy quatrains were an English version
   Of just that rhyme scheme (and God knows what else)
He found in the original in Persian.

★

Lord Byron, seeking out a verse to dally in
   While roaming through *Don Juan*, came to see
The point of imitating the Italian
   Poets back in the sixteenth century:
Don Juan's stanza, jumping like a stallion
   Over its disyllabic rhymes, and free
Of too much room to roam in, came to seem a
Verse pattern all its own *(ottava rima)*.

★

One more famous stanza should be described here;
It can come rhymed, unrhymed, or what you will, at
Least in English, named for the great Greek poet
   Passionate Sappho . . .

Sapphics: four-line stanzas whose first three lines are

Heard—in our hard English at least—as heartbeats,
Then, in one more touch of a final short line,
    Tenderly ending.

★

Rhyme royal is a stanza form of seven
Pentameters, which Chaucer filled with scenes
From *Troilus and Criseyde* and with heaven-
Sent birdsong in the *Parlement*, its means,
More limited than are *The Faerie Queene*'s.
"Royal"?—from a poem by Scotland's first King James.
(Some scholars differ: so it is with names.)

★

A true *Spenserian stanza* wakes up well
With what will seem a quatrain first; in time
The third line rings its "a" rhyme like a bell,
The fourth, its "b" resounding like a dime
In a pay telephone—this paradigm
Demonstrating the kind of interlocking
Of quatrains doubling back on the same rhyme
Ends in an alexandrine, gently rocking
The stanza back to sleep, lest the close be too shocking.

(And so the questions that the last lines ask
The alexandrine answers, as a pleasant task.)

There is a famous way of interlocking tercets:

The unrhymed middle line, in the tight schema
Of tercets spinning out a lengthy text
(Dante gave us this form, called *terza rima*),

Rhymes, after all, with the start of the next
Tercet, then helps set up a new unrhyme
That, sure of foot and not at all perplexed,

Walks across blank space, as it did last time.
(A couplet ends this little paradigm.)

In general,

A *stanza* in Italian means "a room";
    In verse, it needn't keep to square

Corners, as of some dismal tomb,
But wanders anywhere:
Some stanzas can be built of many lines
Of differing length;
Their variation then combines
With rhymes to give it strength.
Along the way
Short lines can play,
And, at the end, a longer and more solemn
Line extends below, a broad base for a column.

Sonnets can be of two general sorts—the so-called
Elizabethan form, with three quatrains and a couplet,
or the Italian kind, with an *octave* rhymed *abba abba*
and a *sestet* of various groupings of *cde*. Here are the
two types:

The kind of *sonnet* form that Shakespeare wrote
—A poem of Love, or Time, in fourteen lines
Rhymed the way these are, clear, easy to quote—
Channels strong feelings into deep designs.
Three *quatrains* neatly fitting limb to joint,
Their lines cut with the sharpness of a prism,
Flash out in colors as they make their point
In what logicians call a syllogism—
(If A, and B, then C)—and so it goes,
Unless the final quatrain starts out "But"
Or "Nevertheless," these groups of lines dispose
Themselves in reasoned sections, tightly shut.
The final couplet's tight and terse and tends
To sum up neatly how the sonnet ends.

*

Milton and Wordsworth made the sonnet sound
Again in a new way; not with the sighs
Of witty passion, where fierce reason lies
Entombed in end-stopped lines, or tightly bound
In chains of quatrain: more like something found
Than built—a smooth stone on a sandy rise,
A drop of dew secreted from the sky's
Altitude, unpartitioned, whole and round.

The *octave*'s over; now, gently defying
Its opening tone, the *sestet* then recalls
Old rhythms and old thoughts, enjambed, half-heard
As verses in themselves. The final word,
Five lines away from what it rhymes with, falls
Off into silence, like an echo dying.

There have been other slight variations on fixed
sonnet patterns, some of them—like film stars that
are shaped by, and shape, their roles—informing and
being blooded, at once, by major poetic occasions.

Another sonnet form, though hardly shocking,
Presents us with three quatrains, like the rest,
But runs the rhymes into an interlocking
Pattern that asks the poet for his best
As each new quatrain puts him to the test
(Or, her, as the case often is), by way
Of having at such moments to divest
Himself of rhyme-words waiting, an array
Of crowded sounds he'd treasured up all day.
No need for noisy ingenuities,
Though; one needs but two rhymes on *d* and *a*
(-*Ay*'s the last *c*-rhyme: there were four of these.)
Such lines that intertwine, like cooked spaghetti,
Were used by Spenser in his *Amoretti*.

Milton once composed a "tailed sonnet" of twenty
lines:

After the sestet of a sonnet, six
More lines are added, playing more than tricks,
          And thereupon we fix
Two shorter, caudal lines that cannot fail
To drag it out; we hammer on a nail
          And thereby hangs a tail,
But I'll not tell it now; instead, we'll call
It quits, and close in couplet after all.

          *

And as for *Modern Love*, George Meredith,
Who brooded most ironically upon it,

Used an extended variant of the sonnet
To do his sad demystifying with
(Of Eros, and of Hymen, God of marriage,
Who, to the sound of flagrant, wailing willows
And low reproaches muttered on the pillows,
Descended in an armor-plated carriage).
Behold the form that disillusion takes!
The *abba* quatrain of the old
Italian mode, its stories oversold,
Goes rambling past the point at which it breaks
Off, and the sestet finishes. Unsweet
Sixteen, this sonnet-pattern might be named,
Ending in embers where once passion flamed,
Sadder and wiser and not half so neat.

*

One final recent variant of sonnet form works
Its way purely syllabically,* in unrhymed lines
Of thirteen syllables, and then squares these off with one
Less line in the whole poem—a thirteener-by-thirteen.
But hidden in its unstressed trees there can lurk rhyming
Lines like these (for instance); as in all syllabic verse
Moments of audible accent pass across the face
Of meditation, summoning old themes to the fair
Courtroom of revision, flowing into parts of eight
And five lines, seven and six, or unrhymed quatrains,
Or triplets, that like this one with unaligned accents
Never jingles in its threes or imbecilities.
Then the final line, uncoupled, can have the last word.

Before we examine some of the more extended
traditional forms, we might consider the working of
other systems of verse listed on page 5. *Pure accentual*
meter, which we all know from the first oral poetry
we hear—nursery rhymes and so forth—measures
stressed syllables only:

In ac*cen*tual *me*ter it *does*n't *mat*ter
*Whe*ther each *line* is *thin* or *fat*ter;

---

*See the next page for why this line doesn't seem to scan.

What you *hear* (this *matters more*)
Is *one, two, three, four*.

In medieval times,

The oldest English   accented meter
Of four, unfailing,   fairly audible
Strongly struck   stresses seldom
Attended to anything   other than
Definite downbeats: how many dim
Unstressed upbeats   in any line
Mattered not much;   motion was measured
With low leaps   of alliteration
Handily harping on   heavy accents
(Echoing equally   all vowels,
Consonant cousins   coming together).

The spirit of purely accentual verse was summoned up by an eminent Victorian:

Sprung rhythm is modern accentual, counting the downbeats.
Instead of pentameter, Gerard Manley Hopkins' verse
Rains down in no shower, but as the sound of a town beats
Down on the ear in a queer-clear way; his terse
Compound words, noun-to-noun-tethered, togethered with
    strange
Wordings (not absurdings) roamed his rhythms' range.

★

Verse called *skeltonic*
Is not cacophonic;
Jiggly and jumpy,
Loose, somewhat lumpy,
Pleasing or prating,
Graceful or grating,
It's always elating,
Often alliterating
Short lines, and neat,
With double downbeat
(Don't scan them in "feet")
Whose rhymes repeat
Forever—no feat

When the measure's meet—
Mixed in with lines like these,
Clearly accented in threes,
Named for John Skelton,
Scholar-poet who dwelt in
Diss, Norfolk, and then
Paraded his pen
To great reknown
In London town
(Born, as far as we know,
In 1460 or so,
Did this world resign
In 1529).
Such lines, so crammed,
Would be doubly damned
Before being enjambed,
Their line-endings lopped,
Criminally cropped
With syntax dropped.
They are all end-stopped.
A skillful skeltonic
May be macaronic.*

Pure syllabic verse—sometimes called "isosyllabic"—
is an importation into English from other languages.
Its lines can be of any length.

Whereas iambic verse will let you hear
Five downbeats, countable inside your ear,

*(In Latin, *id est*,
A magpie's nest
Of languages various,
Stern or hilarious:
Deutsch and *Français*
Together can play
In this wanton way
With *la lingua Italiana*,
Hoy y mañana
When readers understand 'em:
Quod erat demonstrandum.)

Lines made up of ten syllables purely
Without any arrangement of downbeats
Will not seem to be in any meter,
And rhyme becomes something this form defeats.

Thus decasyllabic verse in French or
Japanese, unaccented, will sound like
Something strange to English ears, which still lust
For downbeats, drumbeats (*something*) in a line,
A last syllable at least, stressed, which hits
The nail of a rhyme-word: thus rhyme limits,—
If we are to *hear* it (not as above)—
Pure syllabic wandering. W.
H. Auden and Marianne Moore both wrote
In syllabic meter like this, which can
Always regain a pure *iambic* voice
By sorting out the accents in its words
In any line, or rush into hiding
Again, in caves of accentless shadow.

★

> And stanzas made
>   up of lines
> of varying length
>   like this one—
> with four, three, five, three, six
> syllables, and then one of eight—

>   are quite clearly
>   of the same
>   form as each other;
>   but only
>   the counting eye can tell:
> You use your fingers, not your ear.

One conventional pure syllabic form, borrowed from
Japanese poetry, has been popular in English verse
for over twenty years:

Haiku, with seven
Syllables in between two
Shorter lines of five,

Gently—like cherry
Blossoms in a breeze—allude
To just one season

Sometimes: they are a
Peculiarly Japanese
Form of epigram.

In them, brevity
Lights up with significance
Like a firefly.

The *cinquain* in older French verse was any kind of
five-line stanza. But in English,

Cinquains
Have lines of four
Syllables, six, and eight,
Ending, as starting, with a line
Of two;

But when
Iambs align
To the trained ear these seem
To form a line of twelve, and then
Of ten.

Cinquains
In English verse
Were devised by a bard
Whose name (alas!) was Adelaide
Crapsey.

Accentual-syllabic, pure accentual, and pure syllabic verse all count or measure units—either syllables or just accented ones or both—to determine a
line. But various kinds of unmeasured verse exist,
and have for ages. The most influential of these is
the verse form of the Hebrew Bible, as it was translated into English and thereby resonated throughout
the language in quotation, allusion, and echo.

The verse of the Hebrew Bible is strange; the meter of Psalms
   and Proverbs perplexes.
It is not a matter of number, no counting of beats or syllables.
Its song is a music of matching, its rhythm a kind of
   paralleling.
One half-line makes an assertion; the other part paraphrases
   it; sometimes a third part will vary it.
An abstract statement meets with its example, yes, the way
   a wind runs through the tree's moving leaves.
One river's water is heard on another's shore; so did this
   Hebrew verse form carry across into English.

Modern *free verse*, influenced by the inventiveness
of Walt Whitman in English (and Arthur Rimbaud
among others in French), can be of many sorts; since
a line may be determined in almost any way, and
since lines may be grouped on the page in any fashion, it is the mode of variation itself which is sig-
nificant. Here are examples of a number of different
types:

Free verse is never totally "free":
It can occur in many forms,
All of them having in common one principle—
Nothing is necessarily counted or measured
(Remember biblical verse—see above).
One form—this one—makes each line a grammatical unit.
This can be a clause
Which has a subject and a predicate,
Or a phrase
Of prepositional type.
The in-and-out variation of line length
Can provide a visual "music" of its own, a rhythm
That, sometimes, indented lines
                                        like diagrammed sentences
Can reinforce.
Our eye—and perhaps in a funny, metaphorical way, our
   breath itself—
Can be dragged far out, by some rather longer line, across
   the page,

Then made to trip
On short lines:
The effect is often wry.
Yet such verse often tends
To fall very flat.

★

Another kind of free verse can play a
sort of rhythmic tune at the end
of lines, moving back and forth from those that stop
to those that are enjambed as
sharply as that first one.
Aside from the rhythmic tension
Of varying the ebb and flow of
sense along the lines, of making them seem
more (like this one), or less, like measured lines
(like this
one), this sort of free verse can direct our attention
as well as any iambic line, for
instance, to what our language is made up of:
it can break up compound words at line-ends, sometimes
    wittily,
(like someone talking in winter of a whole hiber-
nation of bears)
like tripping hurriedly over what, when you look
down, turns out to have been a grave
stone.

★

Some free verse is arranged in various
graphic patterns like this that suggest
the barely-seen but silent ghost of a
        classical verse form

like a fragment of Sapphic . . .

★

Free verse can, like a shrewd smuggler, contain more
Measured kinds of line, hidden
inside its own more random-seeming
ones; and when a bit of song
comes, blown in on a kind of wind, it will move

across my country
'tis of thee, sweet land
of liberty,
of thee
I sing—the accented verses get cut up
by line breaks that reveal something about them we'd
never seen before: it's a little
like putting a contour map over a street plan
(Customs inspector: are you
trained to hear heroic couplets beating
on the ear if they are hidden in the linings
of free verse, as in the case of these above?)

★

Free verse can build up various
stanzalike units without
rhyme or measured line length to hold
them together, but the power of blank

space between them marks out their rhythms
as surely as the timing of some iambic clock
but, of course, silently: the
ear alone can't tell where they end.

★

Free verse can be a way of making lines that surge
With a power of rhythmic motion, pulsing and oceanic, then
Break, as if a jetty of tumbled boulders had thrust a long
     finger out into the
Surf, making the rumble of water irregular, keeping
The lines from becoming too ⁻
Metrical, marked with the yardstick
Of dactyls.

★

A milder kind
of *vers libre*
as it was called
earlier in this century

Hardly ever enjambed its lines,
but used the linear unit

and even stanzalike
gatherings of lines
as a delicate way of controlling,
of slowing
the pace of the reading eye
or speeding it up across the page again.

It could single out
words
and hang them in lines all their own
Like sole blossoms on branches,
made more precious
by their loneliness.

*

      And to be able to wander, free
                    (in a wide field, as it were)
verse can amble about
    on a kind of nature walk
           the lines following no
      usual path, for
      then the poem might seem
      to have wandered into
    another kind of meter's backyard
                  but
                      sometimes
            seeming
              to map out the syntax,
                  sometimes
        seeming to do almost the
              opposite,
    this kind of meandering verse can
              even
oddly
        come upon a flower
        of familiar rhythm
             a sight for sore
    ears, or encounter
          a bit later
on,
      once again a patch of

```
        trochees growing somewhere
                                (like an old song)
                                              and
        take one by the
                        stem
            and
                    break
            it
                off
```

And, finally, a unique kind of rhymed free verse, but of a sort that really can only be considered as antiverse:

> Because light verse makes meter sound easy,
> And because saying something just for the rhyme is inept
>   and, well, cheesy,
> Even when you spice up rhyme
> With jokes about sagely beating thyme
> (Although *that* line is more compelling
> As a joke about English spelling)
> A famous comic writer whose name follows developed a
>   deliberate and highly skilled method of writing lines that
>   didn't even try to scan so that the general effect was of
>   a metrical hash:
> Ogden Nash.

One formal aberration has reappeared from time to time, in the Hellenistic age, in the Renaissance, and in modern decades. The so-called *pattern-poem* (or "shaped verse" or, as Guillaume Apollinaire referred to his own French exercises, "calligrammes") is composed in, or typographically arranged in, shapes of images of objects or abstract forms, from some aspect of which the poem's "subject" or occasion will arise. An instance of a sort that is composed directly, rather than arranged by a compositor after being written, is this:

```
                    This is
                a macrodot-shaped
               poem by which we mean
              not merely a disc or an
             emblematic circle which a
            text so figured might claim
           meant sun moon world eternity
          or perfection No Just a blown
          up dot in lines of 7 up to 29
          letters Past the middle the
            lines of type get shorter
             and move faster but all
              adding up to too much
                fuss about making
                   a point
```

A Renaissance version of an ancient adage char-
acterized poetry as speaking picture, and art as mute
poesy. Poetic form can try to avoid the ear by hiding
more and more in its visual areas. Pattern-poems are
the most extreme instance of this that we have seen.
But *concrete poetry*, a development in graphic art of
the past thirty years or so (but developing from typographical experimentation going back to Mallarmé
in the later nineteenth century) depends upon unique
drawn, printed, or assembled representations of patterned inscription, punning rebus, etc. It most often
cannot be read aloud the way all verse can (no matter
how framed or commented-upon by visual aspects
of its meter). Consider, for example, a little concrete
poem I might call "On Touching Sunsets"·

```
              c c
              u u
```

The reading ("To see's to use"—2c's, 2u's) makes a
crepuscular epigram about the use and misuse of
nature. This case is more translatable into speech

than most; the self-descriptive example prepared for
this volume is, alas, too heavy for these light pages.
I include not it, but instructions for realizing it; having followed same, readers will also realize why I
have not burdened them with the actual example.

"Concrete Poem" by John Hollander is to be found in the
keeping of the Yale University Press. It *is* (rather than, as
in the case of real verse or prose, being "inscribed upon,"
"written across," etc.) a concrete slab, 2′ × 2′, heavily
scuffed, scarred, rubbed—its surface texture very rough,
cobwebbed, and active. Discernible upon it are inscribed
words, disposed as represented below. The poem's surface
is such that the last three letters of the word "texture" recede
into its texture. Needless to say, the illustration given here
is not, nor can ever be, the concrete poem. And just as well.

Repetition is a powerful and diversified element of formal structures. It is also a very ancient one: primitive work songs, or prayers, or danced rituals, all involved a solo singer or leader, who would chant new and developing material, and a chorus, who would repeat some shorter element over and over as a kind of punctuation of the new material. Before considering refrains and other modern kinds of repetition, we should distinguish between this primitive but continuing kind of solo-chorus structure and the vastly complex pattern of the Greek choral ode, whether used in tragedy or in public ceremonies. Although Greek verse, as we shall see shortly, used a system of syllable lengths rather than stressed accents, you can see what a typical pattern was like:

The *choral ode*
in ancient Greece was more
than just a verse form: for each section
(like this one), called a *strophe*
was sung—not recited—and danced,
and the dancers were singers.
These words to their music moved
with the dancers in one direction,
then finished their pattern
at the end of part of what they had to say.

The second part
of every section then
would have the same tune, the same rhythm,
the strophe had, and therefore
the whole *antistrophe* would move
with a parallel motion.
(This matching of verse to verse
is referred to as *contrafactum*.)
The dancers moved back then
as they sang with those same steps the other way.

And then a last, unmatching section
called an *epode*, or standing,

followed the strophe (or "turn")
and the antistrophe (or "counterturn")
and, rather more simply, perhaps,
completed the *triad* or section
of which there could be one or several.

But "ode" has another sense, that of a neoclassical
lyric in some accentual-syllabic verse scheme perhaps
adapted from Horace. So:

Pindar's public, grand to-do
Andrew Marvell contracted to
        The semi-private mode
        Of his "Horatian Ode";

The rhyming first and second lines
Of this compactest of designs
        Are followed everywhere
        By a much shorter pair.

A consideration of the whole matter of neoclassical
form might be prefaced by some brief observations
about *quantitative verse*. Greek meter was based on
syllabic quantities, rather than contrasting stresses;
one long syllable (so determined by the length of the
vowel, and by a few positional rules) was set equal
to two short ones, like half notes and quarter notes
in musical notation. A *foot* in quantitative scansion
was like a musical measure: a dactyl was like one of
4/4 time that could have either two half notes, or a
half and two quarters (that is, a dactyl, — ∪∪ , or
a spondee, — —). In Latin, where spoken words
tended to have a stress accent on the penultimate
syllable, following the Greek rules which observed
no word accent (but instead placed a musical downbeat on the long syllable in a foot or bar) made for
some phonetic confusion.

We are concerned only with English verse, however, and its attempts to "imitate" classical meters.
Even more than in Latin, stress dominates English
grammar and syntax, and in order to set up classical
verse forms in English, some kind of metaphoric
version of them had to be framed before poets of the
Renaissance and later, yearning for the voice of an-
tiquity, could imitate them in stressed, romance-
trained English.

One early solution was to assign to English vowels
the length of the analogous ones in Greek or Latin,
and count any syllable "long" that was followed by
two adjacent consonants. Audible stress-accent was
discounted. And thus, in these putatively "quantitative" dactyllic hexameters,

> Āll sūch sȳllāblēs arrang'd in thē clāssǐcāl ōrder
> Cān't bĕ aŭdǐblē tŏ English ears thăt āre tūn'd tŏ ăn āccent
> Mārk'd bў ă pāttērn ōf strēss, nōt bў ă quāntǐtătǐve crăwl.

These lines "scan" only if we show that the pattern
of "long" and "short" syllables falls into the classical
"feet," or musical measures. The inaudibility of these
quantities in any language that had stressed syllables
was a factor in Latin verse; stressed syllables could
either be placed in the positions of long ones, or not.
In the former case, they are called (using the terminology of one modern scholar)

> hómodyne | dáctyls

In the latter case, heterodyne. Stressed syllables

> Soŭndĕd oút | eăch line's | énd ĭn | Vírgǐl's | tērmǐnăl | āccĕnts.

Later on, classical adaptations tried less to be so

literal, and replaced the classical feet, or measures
of longs and shorts, with paired or trined stressed
and unstressed syllables. Thus, the classical iamb,
or short-long, became the English one, or da-*dum*.
Some eighteenth-century German poets wrote in accentual elegiac couplets,

> First a hexameter stretching its dactyls across to a cadence,
>   Then the pentameter line follows and falls to a close.

Accentual versions of stanza forms also occur. We
have come across the accentual sapphic already (page
17). Another strophic type, named for the Greek poet
Alcaeus, was adapted by Horace and then imitated
from him:

> This tight alcáic stánza begíns with a
> Matched pair of longer lines that are followed by
>   Two shorter ones, indented *this* way,
>   Making the meter declaim in English.
>
> So ghosts of ancient structures survive even
> Slow ruin: alcaics somehow outlasted the
>   Greek poets, Roman ones, and Germans
>   (Hölderlin, Klopstock) who made it modern.

Ultimately, modern quatrain forms of two longer,
followed by two shorter, lines are all implicit versions
of this stanza (see the so-called Horatian Ode stanza
of Andrew Marvell, page 34).

> One more version of "classical" stressed meter
> Called *hendecasyllabics* (which is Greek for
> Having syllables numbering eleven)
> Starts right out with a downbeat, always ending
> Feminine, with a kind of hesitation
> Heard just after the pair of syllables (the
> Fourth and fifth ones) which give the line its pattern.

Three stressed syllables sometimes open up this
Line, which, used in Latin by carping Martial
(Even more by fantastical Catullus)
Still holds on to its old, upbraiding cadence.

And this is as good a place as any for two kinds of
tricky device, both neoclassical in origin:

Acrostic verse ("top of the line," in Greek)
Conceals, in a linguistic hide-and-seek,
Readable messages, gems sunk in fetters—
Only read down the lines' initial letters.
Sometimes a loved name here encoded lies:
This instance names itself (surprise, surprise!)
Indeed, these final lines, demure and winning,
Confirm the guess you'd made near the beginning.

Descending from Alexandrian times through the
eighteenth century, a witty device known usually as
echo verse would simulate the syllabic repetitions and
truncations of natural echoes for satiric effect:

Echo will have it that each line's last word
(ECHO:)   *Erred.*
Echo will chop down words like "fantasize"
(ECHO:)   *To size.*
Out of what stuff is Echo's wit then spun?
(ECHO:)   *Pun.*
Can English have a full, Italian echo?
(ECHO:)   *Ecco!*

We shall now return to the matter of repetition.
One kind of medieval European dance song was
called a *carol*, or ring dance. In a carol, the leader
would sing the stanzas, and the dancers the refrain
or *burden:*

The dancers flutter about
Like a circle of fluttering birds,
The leader stands in place

And remembers many more words.
  Birdily, birdily bright
  Their burden is very light.

The dancers circle about
Like a ring around the moon,
Their singing a kind of dance,
Their language a kind of tune.
  Birdily, birdily bright
  Their burden is very light.

Like grain when it is threshed,
Like hay when it is mown,
Making, instead of more sense,
A music of its own:
  Birdily, birdily bright
  Their burden is very light.

A literary lyric poem is a song only metaphorically; it is designed to be spoken or read, and a formal refrain can often serve as a kind of reminder or substitute for an earlier relation to music. Some refrains are literal imitations of music—"fa la la la la," etc. Others may be a thematic phrase or sentence; the structural richness of refrains in modern verse depends upon one simple phenomenon: repeating something often may make it *more trivial*—because more expected and therefore carrying less information, as an engineer might put it—or, because of shifting or developing context in each stanza preceding, *more important.*

What once was called a burden
Was seldom heavy to bear.
It was sung by the dancers, and heard in
Between the stanzas, like air
Rushing by between cars of a train,
Again and again and again.

Like the point of a sharpened tool
Blunted by too much use,
Or a lesson learned in school
Drummed into the obtuse,
Here comes the old refrain
Again and again and again.

Like a sound from the distant past
Of remembered waves on a shore,
Each echo means more than the last,
Once more, once more and once more.
But *less* is more: too much is pain
Again and again and again.
(Like the pounding of hard rain
Again and again and again.)

(Bored with this dulling song,
Clever stanzas may set
Out on a walk less long,
Shift their burdens, and get
Each time, with the old refrain,
A gain and a gain and a gain.)

A BRIEF DIGRESSION: The three-beat accentual rhythm
of the last example reminds one of a problem men-
tioned at the beginning of this discussion, metrical
ambiguity. Keats's line "How many bards gild the
lapses of time" was given as an example; this latest
example of refrain suggests another, reminding us
how

Some lines like houses will—for ill or good—
Take on the look of a whole neighborhood,
Clearing muddles in which, alone, they stood.

As before, when we said a refrain
"Rushes by between cars of a train"—
All the anapests in it rang out
At the other ones gathered about.

But context governs, and will always reign:

"Rushing by between cars of a train"
Becomes a five-beat line without much pain.

But back to repetition. Two well-known forms, one
from medieval Provence, one from France, delighted
nineteenth-century makers of intricate verse and became important forms for meditative speculation in
modern poetry. First, the *villanelle:*

This form with two refrains in parallel?
(Just watch the opening and the third line.)
The repetitions build the villanelle.

The subject thus established, it can swell
Across the poet-architect's design:
This form with two refrains in parallel

Must never make them jingle like a bell,
Tuneful but empty, boring and benign;
The repetitions build the villanelle

By moving out beyond the tercet's cell
(Though having two lone rhyme-sounds can confine
This form). With two refrains in parallel

A poem can find its way into a hell
Of ingenuity to redesign
The repetitions. Build the villanelle

Till it has told the tale it has to tell;
Then two refrains will finally intertwine.
This form with two refrains in parallel
The repetitions build: The Villanelle.

The other such form is the *sestina:* six stanzas, each
of six lines, and a three-line *envoy* (or "send-off"),
the repetition being not of lines, as in the villanelle,
but of the terminal words of the lines of the first
stanza:

Now we come to the complex *sestina:*
In the first stanza, each line's final word

Will show up subsequently at the ends
Of other lines, arranged in different ways;
The words move through the maze of a dark forest,
Then crash out, at the stanza's edge, to light.

The burden of repeating words is light
To carry through the course of a sestina;
And walking through the language of a forest
One comes on the clearing of an echoed word
Refreshingly employed in various ways,
Until one's amble through the stanza ends.

The next one starts out where the last one ends
As in the other cases, with the light
Sounds of two lines, like two roads or pathways
Meeting before they drift apart. Sestina
Patterns reveal the weaving ways a word
Can take through the thick clauses of a forest.

The poet dances slowly through a forest
Of permutations, a maze that never ends
(With seven hundred twenty ways those words
Can be disposed in six-line groups). But light
Falls through the leaves into the dark sestina
Picking out only six clear trails, six ways,

Like change-ringing in bells. The words find ways
And means for coping with an endless forest
By chopping out the course of a sestina.
Walking a known trail sometimes, one emends
The route a bit to skirt a green stone, light
With covering moss; or rings changes on words—

And so it is that the first stanza's word
Order—"Sestina," "Word," "End," and then "Ways"
(Three abstract, three concrete like "Forest," and "Light"
Which interweaves with leaves high in the forest)—
With the words' meanings serving different ends,
Repeats its pattern through the whole sestina.

Now the *envoy*'s last word: as the sestina's
End words make way for curtain calls, in the light
That floods the forest as the whole poem ends.

Some of the lyric forms from France remain a kind of metric dance, without real poetry to say but good for literary play (light verse, *vers de société*).

The *ballade* has only one refrain, but its three full stanzas and short *envoy* are locked to the same rhymes throughout.

Where are the kinds of song that lay
Along the medieval shore
And then moved inland, light and gay,
Still in the ancient garb they wore
When speaking out of bed, and war,
And François Villon's coughs and fleas?
Where is their truth, their mighty roar?
Where are the old ballades like these?

Where are the eight-line stanzas' *a*
bab, the beginning four
Followed by quatrains which convey
The *b*-rhyme that had sung before
Its simple tune, in lines of yore?
Where are the busy final *b*'s
That make the old refrain implore
"Where are the old ballades like these?"

Where are the words that used to play,
Wingèd, among the trees, and pour
Old-fashioned rhyme, they hoped, for aye?
Where's Rostand's rapier wit that tore
Off bits of Cyrano's? Wherefore
Did clever rhyming cease to please?
Since jingle became a crashing bore
Where are the old ballades like these?

ENVOY
Prince of Readers, I've ceased to soar:
With rhymes used up, it's a tighter squeeze.
The *envoy* ("send-off") asks, just once more,
Where are the old ballades like these?

Another French lyric form, the *rondeau*, repeats only

part—the opening two iambic feet, usually—of its
first line:

> The rondeau's French in origin.
> For several centuries it's been
> Of use for light verse, in the main;
> Handling its lines can be the bane
> Of someone with an ear that's tin.
>
> The first words with which we begin
> Return, like a recurring sin—
> More Magdalen's than the crime of Cain.
> (The rondeau's French!)
>
> That's called the *rentrement*; and in
> The course of hearing these lines spin
> Themselves out, one may wait in vain
> For more rhymes, or a full refrain.
> With hardly any loss or gain
> English replaces, with a grin,
> The rondeau's French.

The *triolet* is the briefest of these, 5/8 of it being
composed of its two refrains:

> Triolets' second lines refrain
> From coming back until the end;
> Though the first one can cause some pain
> Triolets' second lines refrain
> From coming back yet once again.
> (The form's too fragile to offend.)
> Triolets' second lines refrain
> From coming back until the end.

The *pantoum* comes, through French again, from
Malay (*pantun*) and is rather like a combination of
villanelle with the unfolding motion of *terza rima* (p.
18). There may be any number of quatrains, but,
starting with the second one, they are generated by
repeating the even-numbered lines of each as the

odd-numbered ones of the next. The final line of the poem repeats the opening one. In addition, a touch of riddle is preserved in that the first half of each quatrain is about something wholly different from the second half. Thus:

> Ever so maddening in the *pantoum*,
> The repetitions frame a subtle doom.
> Evening has entered, her patches of gloom
> Now settled in the corners of the room.
>
> The repetitions frame a subtle doom:
> Each quatrain's first and third lines are refrains;
> Now settled-in, the corners of the room
> Attend the coming fever's chills and pains.
>
> Each quatrain's first and third lines are refrains,
> Returning from the previous second and fourth.
> Attend the coming fever's chills and pains!
> The wind is ominous, and from the north.
>
> Returning from the previous second and fourth,
> All these are complicated here by rhyme.
> The wind is ominous, and from the north—
> We talk about the weather half the time.
>
> All these are complicated here by rhyme
> Cleverly woven on the maker's loom.
> We talk about the weather half the time—
> Ever so maddening!—in the pantoum.

Another form based on refrain: that wonderful modern mode of accentual oral poetry and song called "The Blues." Musically, a 4/4 rhythm, usually slow, moves through twelve measures in a fairly fixed chordal sequence. [Musicians would identify it as I (IV) I IV V I.] The repetition of the first line is not merely decorative, nor expressive, as you will see. Blues are improvised by the singer, like this:

Ballads from Scotland told stories and sang the news—
Ballads from Scotland told stories and sang the news,
   But black America felt and thought the blues.

Now a blues has stanzas, stanzas of a funny kind—
Yes a blues has stanzas of a very funny kind;
   (Do that line again, singer, while you make up your
      mind) . . .

Make up your mind, while the next line gives you time,
Make up your mind, yes, while this line's giving you time,
   Then your train of thought comes running after your
      rhyme.

You can quote a proverb; they say a new broom sweeps
      clean—
Yes, that's what they say: it's the new broom that sweeps
      clean,
   So sing a new line—make that proverb really *mean*.*

You sing the blues upside-down: you begin with the refrain—
O you sing upside-down, you start out with the refrain,
   And the end of a blues is like the falling rain.

—which leads one to remark that

In the words of "standards"—American popular song—
You'll find the germs
Of prosodical terms
Used in a way that sound a little wrong.

This whole introduction, for instance, is called the "verse";
The lines with the tune
That's familiar come soon
But who can remember *this* melody (that's its curse)

                                                   (or worse . . .)

* You see,
   Blues are like weddings, sad as a beat-up shoe
   Blues are like weddings, sad as a beat-up shoe
      With something borrowed, and something old or new.

   Blues are also witty, epigrammatic, and passionate at once.

But now for that A,A,B,A,
The pattern unrolling before us
In a very familiar way:
There are thirty-two bars to the chorus.

Whether crooned by some creature we love
Or by voices that threaten and bore us
Or by neither of the above,
There are thirty-two bars to the chorus.

There's new music for section B;
It's called the "release"—but from what?
—The burden of symmetry?
—The repeated eight bars that it's not?

This paradigm may have a ring
As passé as a big brontosaurus,
But we keep coming back to one thing:
There are thirty-two bars to the chorus.

Of brief, comical forms of verse which have become, in themselves, more like the formats for jokes,
the most celebrated is the *limerick*:

This most famous of forms is a fiddle
That we rub with a sexual riddle;
But the best of a *limerick*—
Though in Dutch or in Cymric—
Are the little short lines in the middle.

★

The mad limericks of one Edward Lear
Took a turn that was rather severe:
Their last rhymes—the same
As their first—were too tame.
That repetitive old Edward Lear!

The *clerihew*, invented by E(dmund) C(lerihew)
Bentley, is a skewed quatrain that frames a way of
turning rhyming jokes on names, and other jokes on
rhymes, and spoofing metrical neatness in the mode
of Ogden Nash (see page 30):

A *clerihew*
Will hardly transport you, or ferry you
Over toward Parnassus
(Better use some poetic Onassis).

Finally, a recent offshoot of the clerihew, invented by Anthony Hecht and first published by him in collaboration with this author: the *double-dactyl* is a pair of quatrains of two accentual dactyllic feet, with the following conditions placed on it:

Starting with nonsense words
("Higgledy-piggledy"),
Then comes a name
(Making line number two);

Somewhere along in the
Terminal quatrain, a
Didaktyliaios*
Word, and we're through.

Or, in a perfect instance,

Higgledy-piggledy
Schoolteacher Hollanders
Mutter and grumble and
Cavil and curse,

Hunting long words for the
Antepenultimate
Line of this light-weight but
Intricate verse.

Before leaving scheme and figure of word and sound, we might remark that there are a number of rhetorical schemes associated with prose as well as with verse. We might consider a few of them that are commonly used in poetry. One of the most fa-

---

*Greek for "composed of two dactyls."

mous, and most important for early poetry, is the
so-called *epic simile*:

> Even as when some object familiar to us all—
> A street, a spoon, a river, a shoe, a star, a toothache—
> Is brought to our attention, called up from our memory
> To light up the darkened surface of something we've barely
>   known of
> —So did the epic simile sing of a silent past.

★

> *Zeugma*'s syntactic punning, sharp and terse,
> As on *in*'s senses, which we now rehearse:
> "Zeugma is used in earnest and this verse."

★

> *Anacoluthon* is a breaking-off
> Of what is being—a syntactic cough.

★

> *Apostrophe!* we thus address
> More things than I should care to guess.
> Apostrophe! I did invoke
> Your figure even as I spoke.

★

> *Anaphora* will repeat an opening phrase or word;
> Anaphora will pour it into a mould (absurd!);
> Anaphora will cast each subsequent opening;
> Anaphora will last until it's tiring.
> Anaphora will seem to batter the hearer's mind,
> Anaphora will make mere likeness seem unkind;
> Anaphora will sound like some rhetorical fault,
> Anaphora will be reformed by Whitman, Walt.
> Or else it can caress you with a gentle hand
> Or else it can be text for hope to understand,
> Or else it can become a kind of incantation,
> Or else it can shape up into a proclamation.

★

> *Homoeoteleuton* is the opposite: like ending,
> Where the same word will make a similar ending

> Or, perhaps, as in Latin, a chunk of case-ending,
> Or, as in English, a participial —ing,
> Or even, if you wish, and perhaps bending
> The usual sense of it, a rhyming sort of ending.

Chiasmus is a general scheme of patterning two pairs of elements; its name is derived from the Greek letter χ (*chi*); in English, we might call it X-ing. Its elements can be merely those of paired vowel-sounds, as in

> Resounding syllables
>
> In simple nouns.

Or the crossing can be one of syntactical elements,

> Echoing adjectives,
>
> And nouns resounding.

Or, muting the funny sound of inversion for modern ears with its archaic and heroic cast, we can do as Milton did, and enjamb the adjectival participle to modify the grammar:

> Echoing adjectives and nouns resounding
> Deep in the draughty vastness of a scheme.

Or the crossing can arrange particular words, as in

> Imagined mirrors mirror imagining

or this:

> Speech which in part reflects on parts of speech

—or even a metaphoric pattern, although here we touch on realms of trope, not scheme; an example which interlaces syntax and image leaves the penultimate word cast as noun and adjective:

> The burning darkness and the *light* freezing.

Other schemes of placement were never classified
by rhetoricians, perhaps because they only came up
in English verse and in the context of English word
order. The way in which a pair of adjectives modi-
fying the same noun can be arranged, for example,
has consequence for our verse. For

> Polysyllabic long words, preceding short ones,
>   deliver
> Adjectival, sharp blows
>   to the
>   modified next noun.

On the other hand, for example, we learn by scan-
ning a pattern of

> Coupled adjectives dynamic,

of their

> Slower disclosure and instructive.

> ★

> Thus, at the end of an iambic line,
> This scheme could find a lasting place, and fine.

We conclude with a general afterthought,

> Let us talk of variation:
> In a very boring meter
> Like this blank (unrhymed) trochaic
> —Four beats, so *tetrameter*—the
> Chance for any subtle rhythm
> To develop, making any
> Line sound much more like itself than
> Like the others all around it
> Isn't very high at all (a
> Cycle written in this verse form
> By the poet Henry Wadsworth
> Longfellow—it's most well known—is
> Called *The Song of Hiawatha*,

Imitated from the Finnish
Meter of an epic cycle
Called—in Finnish—*Kalevala*.)

But let us move into a form—
Iambic, with four beats the norm—
And listen to the way that lines
Tap out their rhythms, while designs
Of rhyme and reason, overlaid
On the straight tune that's being played
Can make these lines (although they rhyme)
Less like a clock that ticks the time
Or wakes us up with an alarming chime.
Lines may be varied with a rare
Misplaced syllable here and there,
Even two beats together, strong
Enough to shove their words along
The line a bit, until they drop
Into the next, and finally stop.
Rhythms can shimmer, just like this;
Two lines can delicately kiss;
Some words' slow burdens make them bleed
And, fudged, bunched, clustered, hurt to read;
Each line can écho what it says;
Yet family resemblances
Still hold between the various faces
Of lines in their respective places.

The effects of sound observed in the preceding lines represent a more general matter, that of so-called "imitative sound" or, more technically, "verbal mimesis." In its own way, this is a kind of myth-making at the smallest level, and can be considered not so much a scheme or pattern, but a mode of trope itself: the myth is one of semantic presence in a place of nonreferential sound (or, as some might want to put it, a natural relation occurring in a conventional one that has, indeed, just been established in the verse). Thus,

Technical mastery should not astound—
The sense must seem an echo to the sound,
And verse can be a charm to conjure up
A ghost of meaning in an empty cup,
That nymph the linguists call "Morpheme"—a naiad
Of sense—from out a cell of sound. This triad:
"The fires of autumn dwindle to December,
A spark of meaning hides in its grey ember
And kindles in its name what we remember"
—Illustrates well the point: nothing in *e*'s
M's and *b*'s means "residual." But these
Are tropes, like rhyme, purporting to have found
In a mere accident of common sound
A hidden jewel of meaning, hard and bright,
Bred by the pressure of the ear's delight.
Thus: *m*-sounds can feel flabbier or firmer
When heard in "mime," or overheard in "murmur";
There's nothing in that general object, *it*,
That suits it for its role in "spit" or "shit"
(Low comedy), or, properly, in "fit."
H's are only breathless when in "hoarse"
("Horses" run smoothly from the start, of course).
Sl as in "slip" and "slap" and "sleet" and "slide"
Etcetera, perhaps connotes a glide
Of unimpeded motion; I suppose
That stuffed, initial *sn* suggests the nose.
But mostly, all these morphophonemes that
Poetry seems to pull out of its hat
Are verse's metaphors of having found
Buried significance in natural ground.

*

Thus, what is not quite "imitative form"
Occurs when roughing up the rhythmic norm
(I've Pope's great lines still pounding in my head)
Gives us a sounding picture of what's said:
Samuel Johnson put the matter right
(He was, as usual, so fiercely bright)—
In order, though, that we can all be sure of
What I've been mentioning, let's take a tour of

A realm in which poems take what form can give—
What Dr. J. called "representative
Versification"—where the sense, profound
Or trivial, seems moved by its own sound.
Let me move here beyond my own example;
Cases from six great poets should prove ample:

For instance, here is Shakespeare's Florizel
(*The Winter's Tale*, Act IV) as he comes to tell
Perdita of his love, and to confess
His wonder at his Princess-Shepherdess,
His language dances—here I am referring
To what's done with the pattern of recurring
Dah diddy dah's: "*When you do dance, I wish you
A wave o' the sea, that you might ever do
Nothing but that*"*—answering moves of phase-
Rhythm and wish and girl and paraphrase.

Like Milton's devils, searching out their curse,
Exploring one line's deadly universe—
"*Rocks, caves, lakes, fens, bogs, dens and shades of death*"†—
We pick our way through nouns with wearied breath.

Dryden's "*harsh cadence of a rugged line*"‡
Where "harsh" roughs up the spondee, can combine
Body of meaning, meter's drapery,
In a wild dance we all can hear and see.

Keats makes us feel the bitter cold, alas—
"*The hare limped trembling through the frozen grass*"§—
Through where three massed stressed syllables define
The slow-dragged footfall of the limping line.
(A similar rhythm wouldn't do at all—
"*The hare skipped briskly . . .*" Though the stresses fall,
And juncture ruptures, in the selfsame places,
That line would not become what it embraces.)

Listen to Tennyson's Elaine: her feet

---

*The Winter's Tale, act 4, sc. 4, lines 140–42.
†*Paradise Lost*, book 2, line 621.
‡"To the Memory of Mr. Oldham," line 16.
§"The Eve of St. Agnes," stanza 1, line 3.

Move down the stairs in a repeating beat
"First as in fear, step after step, she stole
*Down the long tower-stairs, hesitating"**
(In the next line, the spondees' well-played role
And the last word's reversals keep us waiting.)

Chiasms (see page 49) can make
A mirror for a mirroring pool or lake:
In Robert Frost's "Spring Pools," blossoms along
The water's margin see themselves in song—
"These flowery waters and these watery flowers"†—
The mirror made of language becomes ours.

Something more should be said about rhyme in
general, whose nature and function were discussed
on page 14. First, as far as strict, full rhyme is concerned, a warning to versifiers might be extended:

Beware unrhyming nouns like "month" or "orange":
Bad writers mutilate poor words, and mar ing-
Enious measures to provide a rhyme,
Or, perhaps (but this only works one time),
Raise some dead actress, e.g., Una Merkle,
To fit inside the empty-sounding "circle."
Don't build yourself into a rhyming prison
Lest mainsail words get jury-rigged to mizzen;
Don't push your luck too far: rhymes will thin out
After a while even for words like "stout."
Once one has worked through Hebrew names like "Seth"
(Meaning "provided") and "Elizabeth,"
One wearily runs out of rhymes for "breath,"
And, as one must, at last resorts to "death."
So when you've made a point about how "pelf"
Leads back to false attachments to the self,
Stop there, or you'll be on a silly shelf
With an irrelevant Ghibelline or Guelph
Or a dead British actor named George Relph.

*"Lancelot and Elaine," lines 340–41.
†"Spring Pools," line 11.

Sight-rhyme is an anomaly previously noted (page 14), but there are other discrepancies between speech and writing that affect rhyme:

A poet of the seventeenth century
In speaking of a wilderness, might be
Quite humdrum, yet would give us quite a start
By writing of its prospect as "desert"
(Pronounced by him des*art*, though: no trick, this,
Contriving to make rhyming seem amiss
To imitate confusion in the land.
This was a close rhyme, then.) Now, understand,
That as with time, with place: the USA
Has its own dialects, and thus we'd say
Someone from the Midwest, rhyming, would marry
That last word of the line above with "fairy"
(Also for her a homonym with "ferry")
But varying vowels (and "vary" implies not very
Much alike) in East-Coast speech can carry
Varying rhymes: a berry is not named "Barry"
And Harry, balding, is not always "hairy,"
Carrie's is not the sound I grant to Cary,
Etcetera, our rhymes thus sometimes showing
As much of where we're from as where we're going.

Two other sorts of anomaly, both intentional devices of modern poetry, became minor conventions in the twentieth century:

A very nineteen-thirties mode of rhyme
Skewed it a bit, consistently, and used
Last syllables that weren't quite the same

In vowel and consonant; and when pursued
Through interlacings of a formal pattern
(Like *terza rima*, here) last words are poised

Just on the brink of rhyming, and far slanter
Than most—and that this is intentional
And not inept is really quite apparent

(Some clunking rhymes tell more than when they're full).

★

Another recent mode of rhyming's subtle
Adjustments help avoid the jangling rut
Cut by the wheels of an unrolling couplet:
The last stress of a so-called "feminine ending"
Is picked out by a singly rhyming friend
In the next, regularly terminating,
Pentameter—such couplets seem to mate
Two sorts of line, and make the rhyme a trifle
Less obvious (*less artful, more like life,*
You'd ask?—No. Wrong: just making rhyme less ruthless
In its insistence that like sound's like truth.)

Assonance (page 13) is systematic for line-endings
in a medieval narrative verse form:

The epics in Old French ("*Chansons de Geste*")
Such as *The Song of Roland* moved in sets
Of lines like these, with assonance instead
Of full rhyme at the ends of lines, unless
(And this was sometimes just the way it went)
A casual one like this would seem to mess
Up carefully avoided rhyme. Inept?
No. All part of the show. And so we get
These blocks of lines of varying number—"*laisses,*"
They're called—and even if you know no French
You'd guess that they're pronounced like English "less."

These *laisses* could keep on going for a while,
Marking a moment of a story's time,
Glancing around at mountains or at sky,
Noting the sound of many battle-cries
Dying into the silence of the night,
Or framing what some hero in some high
Diction proclaims to someone, as he rides
Into the sunset's all-consuming fire.

Rhyme-pattern has been acknowledged by linear
indentation in typographical conventions from the
sixteenth century to the present:

You may well ask why in successive lines
  Of the same length upon the printed page
One's set flush left, the next one realigns,
  Indented to the right. Not to upstage
The second lines, but to map out the way
  That cross-rhymed lines will line up vertically,
Zig-zagging so that lines which rhyme on *a*
  Will correspond, like those that chime with *b*.

    But then we have to face
      The other case:
   Iambic lines of varied length
   Will be indented differently
Regardless of their rhyming *a, b, c* . . .
    Rhyme having lost its strength
   In governing how lines should run.
   A shorter line, and here I pun,
Will walk one foot behind a longer one
     Though both may rhyme,
     Sing the same song,
    The question of how long
The lines are will determine where they start
Long to the left, and shorter, rightward—rule, not art.

With regard to the indentation of printed poems generally, it might be observed that

Lines of verse can be "flush left," like this
No matter how
Long or short they are, how hit-or-miss
The rhymes are, now
Occurring in commensurate lines or managing to bow
Out at ends of long ones, they
Can all start out like this in the same way.
Or else their left-hand margin can move in
And out by strict rules; here's one, to begin:

[1a]

This mode of indentation all depends
  Not on how long the line is, after all,

But only on the rhyme in which it ends:
    Some lines, against the justifying wall,
Stay in alignment with their rhyming friends
        And others may decide to shun the gloom
        And stand more in the middle of the room.

[1b]

Marianne Moore
indented her syllabic lines
(the first one, four, these next two, eight)
    only when
they "rhymed," albeit in
    their strange way, half-heard and broken
but not according to their length.

[2]

Another way of justifying lines
      Arranged in stanzas takes
   Its cue not from the sound designs
      That rhyming makes
But equal length with equal length aligns;
And one foot shorter, should the poet prune it,
    A line indents itself one unit.
      Like a good tune it
Keeps to the form in which it has been cast.
      Verses like this, each time,
      Will line up (not for rhyme)
      And, in one typical extreme,
      Flush left at last,
A line of six feet (twelve syllables) ends the scheme.

[3]

Couplets flush left: Ben Jonson so prefers
To look like classical hexameters
In epic poems of Virgil or by Homer
"Heroic couplets" thus are no misnomer.

But elegiac couplets, are more fun,
   With a long line and then a shorter one
In Greek or Latin: Ben Jonson could invent
   The English version with just one indent.

—And finally, it should be noted that

Greek and Latin texts, in the age of printing
never marked out lines with initial letters
upper-case, the way that the same editions
    printed in English,

French, Italian, Spanish, or whatsoever,
Marking out the start of lines with clever
Capital letters, saying (redundantly)
Here comes a whole new line again, just see!

Until, just after World War I,
some writers of what was called *vers libre*
or "free verse" (in English) pointedly
refused to capitalize their lines' initial letters
as if to say something
(but what?)
thereby

But here is at least one celebrated case where such
indentation can give the illusion of rhymed groups of
lines where there is no rhyme at all:

How can a sonnet not have rhyme yet keep
   Its name and nature, when its fourteen lines
   Ungrouped by uniforms, or the bright flags
Of marching squadrons, pass in disarray?
How can one make it plain where quatrains end
   When tinkling cymbals and the sounding brass
   Of marching feet whose rhymes repeat have long
Departed down the silent avenue?
Quite easily; Keats wrote an unrhymed one
(*"O thou whose face hath felt the winter's wind"*
  —A thrush speaks both to poet and to reader)

> Clearly, like this one, an Italian sonnet
> (See page 19), octave and sestet marked
> By Syntax, quiet choreographer.

A number of uncommon verse-schemes not previously discussed merit attention, some for the use made of them at times in the past, and some for proving irresistible to important contemporary poets. As a variant of the couplet schemes considered on pages 15–16,

> "Metaphysical" poems and other things
>   Written under the Stuart kings
> Employed another couplet in their day
>   Whose jagged pattern went this way
> As if some Muse (with Lord knows what design)
>   Had stolen from the second line
> A foot: the loud pentameter's report
>   Is ruffled, thus, by something short.
> It seems the couplet will be quite completed,
>   But your prediction gets defeated.

The wonderful fourteen-line Russian form that Pushkin developed for his novel in verse, *Eugene Onegin*, is at once sonnetlike and reminiscent of Byron's *Don Juan*:

> The stanza of Pushkin's *Onegin*
> Unrolls in strict *abab*'s
> Of quatrains (and this rhyme's a plague in
> Lines that are quite as short as these),
> Then a mere couplet seems to break
> The flow of quatrains, but to make
> Adjacent couplets that we call
> A form of quatrain after all.
> Then comes the final way to play
> (In the form we remember from

Tennyson's *In Memoriam*)
A quatrain on rhymes *b* and *a*,
Until at Closure's stern commands, a
Couplet will terminate the stanza.

Among the lyric forms with refrains that come into
English from French, Italian, or Spanish (see pages
40–43) are several kinds of *canzone*. Often an ode-like
form of lines of seven and eleven syllables linked in
rhymes in Italian, the canzone developed in other
forms, such as this maddeningly difficult one. This
sort of extension of the *sestina* (pages 40–41) was
composed by Dante and used in our time by W. H.
Auden and James Merrill, among others:

This form of the *canzone*'s almost too
Taxing to write, because it takes, you see,
Five stanzas of twelve lines, descending to
A last *tornata* of five more that, to
The unobservant eye might seem no more
Difficult than a sestina—maybe two
Sestinas. Wrong. As we sink deep into
Its stanza, there along the bottom lie
The last of the five end-words which ally
Their teams of meaning to give motion to
This painful form (repeating words *hurts* so).
Hereafter we must reap what now we sow.

—These words, I mean. The five words that get so
Familiar, as we go, though one or two
More repetitions still are easy—so
It seems—that, if what one says is so,
Then saying yet once more that what we see
Is what we know, for instance, or that so
Many moments in life are just so-so
And to keep living them again is more
Than we can take, is certainly no more

To be deplored than never saying so.
(Such truisms! But where else does truth lie?
It's not on once-told tales that we rely.)

Well, here we go again. A word like "lie"
Repeated at a stanza's end can so
Becalm a text as almost to say "Lie
Down for a moment, five-stressed line, just lie
Down and relax—don't feel you're coming to
The same bad end again, the usual lie
Against the truth of rhyme, the pail of lye
Flung in the face of variation. See,
Isn't this comfy now? Think of the sea,
Or summer." But "You've made your bed, now lie
In it," the stanzas yet unfinished, more
Out of concern than spite, give warning. More-

over (enjambing even a stanza), more
Terminal words return, those we rely
Upon to cause us trouble, and those more
Likely to entertain us more and more
With their accomplishments (words sing, cook, sew,
Play the piano, warm your bed, and more).
And, like refrains (a raven's "Nevermore,"
A tra-la-lolly beating its tattoo)
Canzone end-words have their music, too,
Affirming music, which in ever more
Recurrent waves, agreeably says, "Si,
Señor" to firmness, as to the shore, the sea.

"Si." "Sea." And here we are now at our C-
Minor triad, sad homecoming, once more.
Each stanza's opening, we've come to see,
Ends with the last one's doubled word. But see,
Beyond these hills of words the end will lie,
The distant water: some more hill, then the sea.
"Thalatta, thalatta!" ("The sea, the sea!")
Weary Greek warriors cried in joy, and so
May we, after another "to" or so,
And moving up and down upon the see-

Saw of our déjà-vu, for an hour or two
Hail that first end-word that we've traveled to.

Canzone, your lines now end with words, *one, two*
(In this *tornata*) *three, four five*: "to," "see,"
"More," "lie," "so"—thus we meet up just once more
(Thirteen times now) with these old friends, and lie
Down to the rest for which we've labored so.
An older form of *canzone* rhymes
Its stanzas rather than its lines.
What can that mean? No final word
In each of these six lines resounds
Until six other lines have passed.
Then a new stanza makes amends.

Then another beginning chimes
With what came first; the verse gives signs
Of weaving schemes that can be heard
Through the following six rounds
Of fancy footwork, moving fast
(Given the weary way it wends).

The tune must return a few more times
As it more tightly intertwines
The stanzas (now we're in the third);
The beat of expectation pounds
More strongly now: the die is cast.
From this point on the course descends

Across plain acres here, or climbs
Cliffs of high diction, where the pines
Cling, crag-held, and the circling bird
Surveys new fields and other grounds
For rhyme's contentions with the vast
Armies of words it apprehends.

(A word alone commits no crimes
Of euphony, nor undermines
Sense, unless its sound's preferred
To all else: then that sound redounds

Against itself, and in a blast
Of tone destroys what it intends

To mean by all its pantomimes.)
Here, though one's ingenuity resigns
Itself to death, what has occurred
Merely in passing still astounds,
Until the final rhyme at last
Marks out where this canzona ends.

The *rondeau* (page 43) has a number of close cousins.
The *rondel* or *roundel*, common in fourteenth- and fif-
teenth-century French and English verse, provided a
musical pattern as well as a textual one:

> *A tercet of refrains takes up a lot*
> *Of room in the roundels that Chaucer wrote,*
> *The third of which would strike the closing note.*
>
> And on a short trip, even, one cannot
> Cram too much cargo into such a boat:
> *A tercet of refrains takes up a lot*
> *Of room in the roundels that Chaucer wrote.*
>
> Even without the music, one knows what
> It means to get a song like this by rote;
> The last return might even seem to quote:
> *"A tercet of refrains takes up a lot*
> *Of room in the roundels that Chaucer wrote,*
> *The third of which would strike the closing note."*

Here is a later form of the roundel that Algernon
Charles Swinburne wrote so many of:

> The roundel ends as it begins; we take
> The first words from the first line, where it bends
> Easily, and with the refrain we make
> The roundel ends.

—But not just yet: its rhyming still extends
Through six new lines before they come awake,
Again, those last few words, those sleeping friends

We started out with and will not forsake;
What though the weary journey's way one wends,
When it is finally time to take a break
      The roundel ends.

One more of these was devised by Jean de la Fontaine, author of the famous *Fables*; it is the *rondeau redoublé*:

The two rhymes of the rondeau redoublé
Appear at once for all to hear and see;
Quatrains like this one speed it on its way,
But each of them pays one line as a fee.

Those first lines will come back in turn, with glee,
To haunt successive stanzas' rooms, and prey
Upon new lines that seek in vain to flee
The two rhymes of the rondeau redoublé.

But each refrain line gets to be passé
Once it has played its game by breaking free
Of that first stanza; once again, here, it may
Appear at once for all to hear and see.

Not like some moral, some decoding key,
Something to sum up what your lines convey—
The next line flows, a river, toward its sea:
Quatrains like this one speed it on its way.

Enter the fourth refrain to help defray
The expense incurred (as it was bound to be);
Now one has learned just what it meant to say
"But each of them pays one line as a fee"

Now that debt's paid, just two more lines of *a*
(In usual rhyme-notation) and of *b*.

We'll end with an echo of that first array
Of burdens, having worked through, from A to Z
   The two rhymes.

One of the accentual adaptations of classical meters (see pages 36–37) was used by romantic poets,
both in German and in English, for narrative poems:

English or German hexameters, beating out stresses instead of
Classical quantities, had their romantic uses: consider
Longfellow's tale of *Evangeline,* using the meter of Goethe's
Hermann und Dorothea (rather than Hölderlin's mighty
Hymn to his ever-adored, distant and ancient Aegean
Moving in similar motions, but not for such homely
   occasions):
This was the meter primeval, the murmuring measure of
   Homer
Heard through the bumpety-bump of Germanic accentual
   patterns.

—And speaking of matters of rhythm rather than
rhyme, we might take note of line-types like the following:

Now as anapests, say, and trochees mingle,
   The sounds of stress move in funny paces;
All the following lines will keep their jingle
   And set their feet in the proper places.

But poetical lines that freeze in sin burn
   In fires of hell, with eternal curses,
When so frequently used by A. C. Swinburne
   (What scholars call *logaoedic* verses).

There are other sorts of meters we could simply call *ad hoc*:
   What's their shape? It takes a moment to descry it,
But the pulsing of their rhythm is as steady as a rock
   By the time two lines or more solidify it.

I should also have said (it went out of my head) back at
   somewhere around page fourteen,
That in internal rhyming a strange sort of timing occurs
   when a line can be seen
As three parts of a whole whose corporate role is to sit
   without rocking the boat,
While the line speeds along in a sequence of song that we
   hear without missing a note.

   (BUT, to break them apart
   Into lines, from the start,
Which, though, shorter, would rhyme at the end,
   Is to alter their shape
   And to let them escape
The corral in which they have been penned.)

Internal rhyme, discussed on page 14, can be either
casual or schematically recurrent. One form of this
arose in the Middle Ages:

Late Latin verse could ensure a re-echoing, where the
   caesura
Chimed—in what's called *Leonine Rhyme*—with the end of
   the line.
"This is the forest primeval . . ." is not necessarily evil
Jingle in English; the form'll remain, though, a little
   abnormal.

Very rare and curious is *rhopalic* verse (from Greek,
"clublike"—expanding or thickening toward the
end). In whatever the meter, the words in the line get
longer as the line moves on, e.g.,

Words along rhopalic pentameters
Add extra syllables, gradually;
While shadows, lengthening, attenuate,
Lines thicken approaching termination.

And now, a few more verse forms from the literatures of non-Western languages that have been
adapted to English. A Japanese verse form older even
than the *haiku* (pages 24–25) is the *tanka*. It has not
developed the international vogue of the former but
nevertheless makes for a syllabic stanza worth playing with, also composed of lines of seven and five:

> Like a *haiku* that,
> Awaking from dreams, dreams on
>   From sleep's closing door,
> The *tanka*'s vision lives on
> For fourteen syllables more.

The French *pantoum* (page 43) seems much more
like a kind of *rondeau redoublé* when we compare it
with its actual Malay precursor, the *pantun*. This is a
single quatrain only, rhyming *abab*. But the sentence
making up the first *ab* has no immediate logical or
narrative connection with the second. Only the
rhyme pattern and some pun or like-sounding con-
struction connects them on the surface. It is only after
the lines have sunk in that the deep connection
emerges. The following example might be entitled
"Catamaran":

> *Pantuns* in the original Malay
> Are quatrains of two thoughts, but of one mind.
> Athwart my two pontoons I sail away,
> While touching neither; land lies far behind.

Ghazals are couplets, also apparently disjunct from
each other, assembled into poems written in Arabic,
Persian, Urdu, and Turkish. Both lines of the first
couplet, and the second lines of all the following

ones, end with a repeated refrain (*Radif*) and, just before that, a rhyming word (*Qafia*). The poet signs his name pseudonymously in the final ghazal.

For couplets, the ghazal is prime; at the end
Of each one's a refrain like a chime: *"at the end."*

But in subsequent couplets throughout the whole poem,
It's this second line only will rhyme at the end.

On a string of such strange, unpronounceable fruits,
How fine the familiar old lime at the end!

All our writing is silent, the dance of the hand,
So that what it comes down to's all mime, at the end.

Dust and ashes? How dainty and dry! we decay
To our messy primordial slime at the end.

Two frail arms of your delicate form I pursue,
Inaccessible, vibrant, sublime at the end.

You gathered all manner of flowers all day,
But your hands were most fragrant of thyme, at the end.

There are so many sounds! A poem having one rhyme?
—A good life with a sad, minor crime at the end.

Each new couplet's a different ascent: no great peak,
But a low hill quite easy to climb at the end.

Two-armed bandits: start out with a great wad of green
Thoughts, but you're left with a dime at the end.

Each assertion's a knot which must shorten, alas,
This long-worded rope of which I'm at the end.

Now Qafia Radif has grown weary, like life,
At the game he's been wasting his time at. THE END.

We conclude with the interlocking couplet scheme
of Vietnamese verse, both folk-poetry and long narrative works like the famous *Tale of Kiều* by Nguyễn
Du. *Lục-bát* ("six-eight," referring to the number of
syllables in each line) also includes syllabic tone in
the pattern, but only the rhyme scheme can be repro-
duced in English adaptation:

> Lục-bát in Vietnamese
> Are couplets just like these: you pen
>   A line of six and then
> A line of eight (not ten) will rhyme
>   With the next six, whose chime
> Echoes yet one more time, inside
>   The next eight—see it bide
> Its time, seeming to hide from view
>   Behind the final two
> Syllables of those few. And so
>   On and on they can go . . .

APPENDIX

his enlarged edition allows me to reprint some examples of the work of my precursors in the mode of formal self-description. First must be Alexander Pope's great representation (from *An Essay on Criticism*) of both metrical ineptitude and functional brilliance in the heroic couplet. Notice how he associates those who judge poetry only by the smoothness and easy vulgarity of its verse ("numbers") with bumbling incompetence: those who are all for metrical style have tin ears, as it were. On the other hand, the effective use of sound as "an echo to the sense" he locates in lines applying to Homeric (*Ajax*) and Virgilian (*Camilla*) moments, rather than to pure self-description without any further subject—the Virgilian alexandrine (see page 11), about skimming along the sea and flying over the fields, is as rapid in its apparent phonological motion as the bad poet's line, only about itself, is slow.

> But most by *numbers* judge a poet's song,
> And smooth or rough, with them, is right or wrong;
> In the bright Muse though thousand charms conspire,
> Her voice is all these tuneful fools admire,

Who haunt Parnassus but to please their ear,
Not mend their minds; as some to church repair,
Not for the doctrine but the music there.
These equal syllables alone require,
Though oft the ear the open vowels tire,
While expletives their feeble aid do join,
And ten low words oft creep in one dull line,
While they ring round the same unvaried chimes,
With sure returns of still expected rhymes,
Where'er you find "the cooling western breeze,"
In the next line, it "whispers through the trees";
If crystal streams "with pleasing murmurs creep,"
The reader's threatened (not in vain) with "sleep."
Then, at the last and only couplet fraught
With some unmeaning thing they call a thought,
A needless Alexandrine ends the song,
That, like a wounded snake, drags its slow length along.
Leave such to tune their own dull rhymes, and know
What's roundly smooth, or languishingly slow;

. . . .

True ease in writing comes from art, not chance,
As those move easiest who have learned to dance.
'Tis not enough no harshness gives offence,
The sound must seem an echo to the sense.
Soft is the strain when Zephyr gently blows,
And the smooth stream in smoother numbers flows;
But when loud surges lash the sounding shore,
The hoarse, rough verse should like the torrent roar.
When Ajax strives, some rock's vast weight to throw,
The line too labours, and the words move slow;
Not so, when swift Camilla scours the plain,
Flies o'er the unbending corn, and skims along the main.

Ben Jonson, pretending to hold a minority English
Renaissance view that rhyme, absent in Greek and
Latin classical poetry, should be banished as a me-
dieval corruption of poetic language, wrote "A Fit of
Rhyme against Rhyme," in which he puns on an older
meaning of "fit" as a canto of a narrative poem.

("Conceit" in line 3 refers to poetic metaphor generally here.)

A FIT OF RIME AGAINST RIME

Rime, the rack of finest wits,
That expresseth but by fits,
     True conceit.
Spoiling senses of their treasure,
Cozening judgment with a measure,
     But false weight.
Wresting words from their true calling;
Propping verse for fear of falling
     To the ground.
Jointing syllables, drowning letters,
Fastening vowels, as with fetters
     They were bound!
Soon as lazy thou wert known,
All good poetry hence was flown,
     And art banished.
For a thousand years together
All Parnassus green did wither,
     And wit vanished.
Pegasus did fly away,
At the wells no muse did stay,
     But bewailed
So to see the fountain dry,
And Apollo's music die,
     All light failed!
Starveling rimes did fill the stage,
Not a poet in an age
     Worth crowning.
Not a work deserving bays,
Nor a line deserving praise,
     Pallas frowning;
Greek was free from rime's infection,
Happy Greek by this protection
     Was not spoiled.
Whilst the Latin, queen of tongues,
Is not yet free from rime's wrongs,

> But rests foiled.
> Scarce the hill again doth flourish,
> Scarce the world a wit doth nourish
>   To restore
> Phoebus to his crown again,
> And the muses to their brain
>   As before.
> Vulgar languages that want
> Words, and sweetness, and be scant
>   Of true measure,
> Tyrant rime hath so abused
> That they long since have refused
>   Other ceasure;
> He that first invented thee
> May his joints tormented be,
>   Cramped forever;
> Still may syllables jar with time,
> Still may reason war with rime,
>   Resting never.
> May his sense when it would meet
> The cold tumor in his feet
>   Grow unsounder.
> And his title be long fool,
> That in rearing such a school
>   Was the founder.

Thomas Campion, taking Jonson's position on rhyme more seriously (although both poets always used it for lyric, elegiac, and satiric verse), composed the following exemplary passage of blank verse about why it must be blank:

> Go, numbers, boldly pass, stay not for aid
> Of shifting rhyme, that easie flatterer,
> Whose witchcraft can the ruder ears beguile.
> Let your smooth feet, inured to purer art,
> True measures tread. What if your pace be slow,
> And hops not like the Grecian elegies?
> It is yet graceful, and well fits the state
> Of words ill-breathèd and not shaped to run.

Go then, but slowly, till your steps be firm;
Tell them that pity or perversely scorn
Poor English Poesy as the slave to rhyme,
You are those lofty numbers that revive
Triumphs of Princes and stern tragedies,
And learn henceforth t'attend those happy sprites
Whose bounding fury height and weight effects.
Assist their labor, and sit close to them,
Never to part away till for desert
Their brows with great Apollo's bays are hid.

Here are two metrical examples from Samuel Taylor Coleridge. The two short ones are themselves adapted from the German poet Schiller, and the longer sequence of hexameters (for which see page 36) is addressed to William and Dorothy Wordsworth.

THE HOMERIC HEXAMETER

Described and Exemplified

Strongly it bears us along in swelling and limitless billows,
Nothing before and nothing behind but the sky and the
ocean.

THE OVIDIAN ELEGIAC METRE

Described and Exemplified

In the hexameter rises the fountain's silvery column;
In the pentameter aye falling in melody back.

HEXAMETERS

William, my teacher, my friend! dear William and dear
Dorothea!
Smooth out the folds of my letter, and place it on desk or
on table;
Place it on table or desk; and your right hands loosely half-
closing,
Gently sustain them in air, and extending the digit didactic,

Rest it a moment on each of the forks of the five-forkéd left
   hand,
Twice on the breadth of the thumb, and once on the tip of
   each finger;
Read with a nod of the head in a humouring recitativo;
And, as I live, you will see my hexameters hopping before
   you.
This is a galloping measure; a hop, and a trot, and a
   gallop!

All my hexameters fly, like stags pursued by the stag-
   hounds,
Breathless and panting, and ready to drop, yet flying still
   onwards,
I would full fain pull in my hard-mouthed runaway hunter;
But our English Spondeans are clumsy yet impotent curb-
   reins;
And so to make him go slowly, no way left have I but to
   lame him.

Here are a number of sonnets on the sonnet. First,
two by Wordsworth: the first of these discusses the
economy of condensation, and how the enclosed
chamber of fourteen lines becomes a place of poetic
meditation and productivity.

Nuns fret not at their convent's narrow room;
And hermits are contented with their cells;
And students with their pensive citadels;
Maids at the wheel, the weaver at his loom,
Sit blithe and happy; bees that soar for bloom,
High as the highest Peak of Furness-fells,
Will murmur by the hour in foxglove bells;
In truth the prison, unto which we doom
Ourselves, no prison is: and hence for me,
In sundry moods, 'twas pastime to be bound
Within the Sonnet's scanty plot of ground;
Pleased if some Souls (for such there needs must be)
Who have felt the weight of too much liberty,
Should find brief solace there, as I have found.

The second one writes the literary history of sonnets, but in a strange way, chronologically speaking: the historical sequence should be Dante, Petrarch, Tasso, Camoëns, Spenser, Shakespeare, Milton. But Wordsworth's ordering reinvents his own personal history, bracketing the order with the greatest English poets and connecting Spenser with Milton as he feels Milton is adjacent to himself.

> Scorn not the sonnet; critic, you have frowned,
> Mindless of its just honours; with this key
> Shakespeare unlocked his heart; the melody
> Of this small lute gave ease to Petrarch's wound;
> A thousand times this pipe did Tasso sound;
> With it Camoëns soothed an exile's grief;
> The sonnet glittered a gay myrtle leaf
> Amid the cypress with which Dante crowned
> His visionary brow: a glow-worm lamp,
> It cheered mild Spenser, called from Faeryland
> To struggle through dark ways; and, when a damp
> Fell round the path of Milton, in his hand
> The thing became a trumpet; whence he blew
> Soul-animating strains—alas, too few!

John Keats's poem is another masterpiece. Notice how he contrives a scheme which keeps rhyming words at least four lines apart (until the final quatrain), even as he moves from the myth of Andromeda chained to a rock to one in which rhyming links move from being chains (like Jonson's fetters) to thongs holding a sandal on, to intertwined laurel in a crown.

ON THE SONNET

> If by dull rhymes our English must be chain'd,
>   And, like Andromeda, the Sonnet sweet
> Fetter'd, in spite of pained loveliness;

Let us find out, if we must be constrain'd,
  Sandals more interwoven and complete
To fit the naked foot of poesy;
Let us inspect the lyre, and weigh the stress
Of every chord, and see what may be gain'd
  By ear industrious, and attention meet;
Misers of sound and syllable, no less
Than Midas of his coinage, let us be
  Jealous of dead leaves in the bay-wreath crown;
So, if we may not let the Muse be free,
  She will be bound with garlands of her own.

Dante Gabriel Rossetti prefaced his sonnet sequence, *The House of Life*, with this remarkable poem.
The octave-sestet distinction (see pages 19–20) is par-
amount here, and the sestet's metaphor of a coin is
not only a minor version of a carved "monument" in
the octave, but itself suggests a head/tail difference.
"A moment's monument" means both a short, mo-
mentary memorial piece and a monument *to* some
moment of intense experience.

A Sonnet is a moment's monument,—
  Memorial from the Soul's eternity
  To one dead deathless hour. Look that it be,
Whether for lustral rite or dire portent,
Of its own arduous fulness reverent:
  Carve it in ivory or in ebony,
  As Day or Night may rule; and let Time see
Its flowering crest impearled and orient.

A Sonnet is a coin: its face reveals
  The soul,—its converse, to what Power 'tis due:—
Whether for tribute in the august appeals
  Of Life, or dower in Love's high retinue,
It serve; or, 'mid the dark wharf's cavernous breath,
In Charon's palm it pay the toll to Death.

Edwin Arlington Robinson's sonnet echoes both
Keats and Rossetti in theirs, although making mani-

fest the relation of maker and thing made, of burden and reward:

SONNET

The master and the slave go hand in hand,
Though touch be lost. The poet is a slave,
And there be kings do sorrowfully crave
The joyance that a scullion may command.
But, ah, the sonnet-slave must understand
The mission of his bondage, or the grave
May clasp his bones, or ever he shall save
The perfect word that is the poet's wand.

The sonnet is a crown, whereof the rhymes
Are for Thought's purest gold the jewel-stones;
But shapes and echoes that are never done
Will haunt the workshop, as regret sometimes
Will bring with human yearning to sad thrones
The crash of battles that are never won.

—And finally, Robert Burns's joyful comic celebration of the fundamental fourteen-ness of sonnethood:

A SONNET UPON SONNETS

Fourteen, a sonneteer thy praises sings;
What magic myst'ries in that number lie!
Your hen hath fourteen eggs beneath her wings
That fourteen chickens to the roost may fly.
Fourteen full pounds the jockey's stone must be;
His age fourteen—a horse's prime is past.
Fourteen long hours too oft the Bard must fast;
Fourteen bright bumpers—bliss he ne'er must see!
Before fourteen, a dozen yields the strife;
Before fourteen—e'en thirteen's strength is vain.
Fourteen good years—a woman gives us life;
Fourteen good men—we lose that life again.
What lucubrations can be more upon it?
Fourteen good measur'd verses make a sonnet.

Of all the French lyric forms (see pages 40–44), it is the sestina which has most fascinated modern poets. Here are three sestinas on the subject of themselves. Edmund Gosse's premodernist poem praises the Provençal poet Arnaut Daniel (addressed in the quoted epigraph as "the first among all others, great master of love [poetry]"), the inventor of the form.

SESTINA

> Fra tutti il primo Arnaldo Daniello
> Gran maestro d'amor.—*Petrarch*

In fair Provence, the land of lute and rose,
Arnaut, great master of the lore of love,
First wrought sestines to win his lady's heart,
Since she was deaf when simpler staves he sang,
And for her sake he broke the bonds of rhyme,
And in this subtler measure hid his woe.

"Harsh be my lines," cried Arnaut, "harsh the woe
My lady, that enthorn'd and cruel rose,
Inflicts on him that made her live in rhyme!"
But through the metre spake the voice of Love,
And like a wild-wood nightingale he sang
Who thought in crabbed lays to ease his heart.

It is not told if her untoward heart
Was melted by her poet's lyric woe,
Or if in vain so amorously he sang;
Perchance through cloud of dark conceits he rose
To nobler heights of philosophic love,
And crowned his later years with sterner rhyme.

This thing alone we know: the triple rhyme
Of him who bared his vast and passionate heart
To all the crossing flames of hate and love,
Wears in the midst of all its storm of woe,—
As some loud morn of March may bear a rose,—
The impress of a song that Arnaut sang.

"Smith of his mother-tongue," the Frenchman sang

Of Lancelot and of Galahad, the rhyme
That beat so bloodlike at its core of rose,
It stirred the sweet Francesca's gentle heart
To take that kiss that brought her so much woe
And sealed in fire her martyrdom of love.

And Dante, full of her immortal love,
Stayed his drear song, and softly, fondly sang
As though his voice broke with that weight of woe;
And to this day we think of Arnaut's rhyme
Whenever pity at the labouring heart
On fair Francesca's memory drops the rose.

Ah! sovereign Love, forgive this weaker rhyme!
The men of old who sang were great at heart,
Yet have we too known woe, and worn thy rose.

Donald Hall's sestina refers to Ezra Pound, who wrote several in imitation of the Provençal (Hall echoes a line of Pound's about *his* precursor Robert Browning), but soon explores the complex questions of repetition, closure, and self-reference set up by a serious sense of the form itself and, in particular, by his chosen end-words.

SESTINA

Hang it all, Ezra Pound, there is only the one sestina,
Or so I thought before, always supposing
The subject of them invariably themselves.
That is not true. Perhaps they are nearly a circle,
And they tell their motifs like party conversation,
Formally repetitious, wilfully dull,

But who are we to call recurrence dull?
It is not exact recurrence that makes a sestina,
But a compromise between a conversation
And absolute repetition. It comes from supposing
That there is a meaning to the almost-circle,
And that laws of proportion speak of more than
themselves.

I think of the types of men who have loved themselves,
Who studious of their faces made them dull
To find them subtle; for the nearly-a-circle,
This is the danger. The introvert sestina
May lose its voice by childishly supposing
It holds a hearer with self-conversation.

When we are bound to a tedious conversation,
We pay attention to the words themselves
Until they lose their sense, perhaps supposing
Such nonsense is at very least less dull.
Yet if the tongue is held by a sestina,
It affirms not words but the shape of the unclosed circle.

The analogy: not the precise circle,
Nor the loose patching of a conversation
Describes the repetition of a sestina;
Predictable, yet not repeating themselves
Exactly, they are like life, and hardly dull,
And not destroyed by critical supposing.

Since there is nothing precise (always supposing)
Consider the spiraling, circular, not full-circle
As the type of existence, the dull and never dull
Predictable, general movement of conversation,
Where things seem often more, slightly, than themselves,
And make us wait for the coming, like a sestina.

And so we name the sestina's subject, supposing
Our lives themselves dwindle, an incomplete circle;
About which, conversation is not dull.

Alan Ansen, another contemporary, brilliantly con-
tracts the line-lengths of successive stanzas in re-
counting the history of the form, until he is left, in
the envoy, or tornata, with only the end-words themselves, as if the shortening of the lines signified the
dwindling of a tradition; the diction and syntax also
move to a colloquial style at the end. Note, too, his
allusion to Ben Jonson's verses (page 71) in his title.

A FIT OF SOMETHING AGAINST SOMETHING

For John Ashbery

In the burgeoning age of Arnaut when for God and man
   to be
Shone a glory not a symptom, poetry was not austere.
Complicated laws it followed, generosity through order,
Dowered acrobats with hoops trapezing laurels undergone.
Fountainlike gyrations earned the free trouvère the name
   of master,
And the climax of his daring was the dazzling sestina.

When love the subject-object of Romance sestina
Left gay Provence for learned Italy to be
The guide and guard and graveyard of a supreme master,
The plaything followed, intricate turned more austere,
And doubled in and on its tracks, now woebegone
Began to learn its place and kiss the rod of order.

Petrarch and Sidney, time's woodsmen, reorder
To pastoral the still pregnant sestina
With history and logic come to be
The inspissations of its present master
Landscapes that turn upon themselves have gone
To shape a shining surface to austere.

The pious young would be austere;
They pant and puff pursuing order
(Within a shorter-breathed sestina
The fewer true). Those that have gone
The masturbatory course must be
In doubt if they or it is master.

New rebels will not master
Forms pointlessly austere.
They feel that they will be
Screwed by that alien order,
That Gestapo sestina,
Cats, it's the most ungone.

Its zing's all gone,
It's no master.
Get lost, sestina,

Go way, austere.
You'll always be
Out of order.

Sestina order,
Austere master,
Be gone!!!

   This little anthology concludes with Swinburne's
splendid roundel, and some light-verse self-descrip-
tions of other lyric forms.

THE ROUNDEL

A roundel is wrought as a ring or a star-bright sphere,
With craft of delight and with cunning of sound unsought,
That the heart of the hearer may smile if to pleasure his ear
     A roundel is wrought.

Its jewel of music is carven of all or of aught—
Love, laughter or mourning—remembrance of rapture or
   fear—
That fancy may fashion to hang in the ear of thought.

As a bird's quick song runs round, and the hearts in us
   hear
Pause answer to pause, and again the same strain caught,
So moves the device whence, round as a pearl or tear,
     A roundel is wrought.

THE RONDEAU

Your rondeau's tale must still be light—
No bugle-call to life's stern fight!
   Rather a smiling interlude
   Memorial to some transient mood
Of idle love and gala-night.

Its manner is the merest sleight
O' hand; yet therein dwells its might,
   For if the heavier touch intrude
     Your rondeau's stale.

Fragrant and fragile, fleet and bright,
And wing'd with whim, it gleams in flight
  Like April blossoms wind-pursued
  Down aisles of tangled underwood;—
Nor be too serious when you write
    Your rondeau's tale.

                        Don Marquis

VILLANELLE

A dainty thing's the Villanelle.
  Sly, musical, a jewel in rhyme,
It serves its purpose passing well.

A double-clappered silver bell
  That must be made to clink in chime,
A dainty thing's the Villanelle;

And if you wish to flute a spell,
  Or ask a meeting 'neath the lime,
It serves its purpose passing well.

You must not ask of it the swell
  Of organs grandiose and sublime—
A dainty thing's the Villanelle;

And, filled with sweetness, as a shell
  Is filled with sound, and launched in time,
It serves its purpose passing well.

Still fair to see and good to smell
  As in the quaintness of its prime,
A dainty thing's the Villanelle,
It serves its purpose passing well.

                        W. E. Henley

TRIOLET

Easy is the Triolet,
  If you really learn to make it!
Once a neat refrain you get,
Easy is the Triolet.
As you see!—I pay my debt
  With another rhyme. Deuce take it,

Easy is the Triolet,
  If you really learn to make it!
                       W. E. Henley

THE TRIOLET

Your triolet should glimmer
  Like a butterfly;
In golden light, or dimmer,
Your triolet should glimmer,
Tremble, turn, and shimmer,
  Flash, and flutter by;
Your triolet should glimmer
  Like a butterfly.
                    Don Marquis

PATTERNS IN PRACTICE

his is a little exhibit of the patterns played with in the previous pages as they are worked with in actual poetry. They are given as listed in the index to this book, in alphabetical order, and each is keyed to the page or pages in the preceding text wherein it is discussed. Because of limitations of space, I have had to quote at minimal length, although in the case of poetic forms (sonnet, sestina, etc.) I have of course given whole poems. In the case of certain patterns—e.g., blank verse, Spenserian stanza—I have given a range of examples to demonstrate the modulation of the form across poetic history. The passages of "verbal mimesis" are more extended than those quoted and analyzed in verse in the main body of the text. But these examples are, like all the others, unglossed, and readers will consider for themselves what is going on in them, mimetically speaking. What the significance of the use of any of these forms or devices might be for a particular literary period, a particular poet, and a particular poem, are the subject of literary criticism and history. Some of these questions may be inferred, however, from comparing these examples with others appearing in one's subsequent reading.

ACCENTUAL METERS pp. 21–23

Couplets of two beats

One, two
Buckle my shoe.
Three, four
Shut the door . . . etc.
                    [Anonymous, nursery rhyme, ca. tenth century, C.E.]

Older English four beats, unrhymed

Injured by iron, I am a loner
Scarred by the strokes of the sword's edge;
Wearied of battle war I behold,
The fiercest foes, yet I hope for no help.
                    *[Anonymous, Old English eighth century,
                    riddle (a shield), translated by John Hollander]*

My deuce, my double, my dear image,
Is it lively there, that land of glass
Where song is a grimace, sound logic
A suite of gestures? You seem amused.
How well and witty when you wake up,
How glad and good when you go to bed,
Do you feel, my friend? What flavor has
That liquor you lift with your left hand . . .
                    [W. H. Auden, The Age of Anxiety, *1947]*

Couplets of four beats

There is not wind enough to twirl
The one red leaf, the last of its clan,
That dances as often as dance it can
Hanging so light, and hanging so high
On the topmost twig that looks up to the sky.

Hush, beating heart of Christabel!
Jesu, Maria shield her well!
She folded her arms beneath her cloak,
And stole to the other side of the oak.
                    [Samuel Taylor Coleridge, Christabel I, *1797]*

Quatrain of three beats

It was down in old Joe's bar-room
In a corner by the Square,
They were serving drinks as usual,
And the usual crowd was there
>   *[Anonymous, "St. James Infirmary," ca. 1900]*

All dripping in tangles green,
Cast up by a lone sea,
If purer for that, O Weed,
Bitterer, too, are ye?
>   *[Herman Melville, "The Tuft of Kelp," 1888]*

Quatrain of six, five, six, five beats

If I pass during some nocturnal blackness, mothy and warm,
    When the hedgehog travels furtively over the lawn,
One may say, "He strove that such innocent creatures should
        come to no harm,
    But he could do little for them; and now he is gone."
>   *[Thomas Hardy, "Afterwards," 1917]*

Unrhymed lines of seven beats

It is an easy thing to triumph in the summers sun
And in the vintage to sing on the waggon loaded with corn
It is an easy thing to talk of patience to the afflicted . . .
It is an easy thing to laugh at wrathful elements
To hear the dog howl at the wintry door, the ox in the
    slaughter house moan
To see a god on every wind and blessing in every blast
To hear the sounds of love in the thunder storm that destroys
    our enemies house
To rejoice in the blight that covers his field, & the
    sickness that cuts off his children
While our olive & vine sing & laugh round our door & our
    children bring forth fruits and flowers
>   *[William Blake, The Four Zoas, 1796–1807]*

ACCENTUAL HEXAMETERS pp. 36, 73–74

Loe, I doe heare Godds temple, as erst, so againe be
    frequented,
And we within thy porches againe glad-wonted abiding,
Lovely Salem shall find: thou Citty rebuilt as a Citty,
Late disperst, but now united in absolute order.
Now there shalbe the place for God's holy people
    appointed.

> [*Mary Sidney*, "*Psalm 122* Laetatus Sum," *ca. 1590*]

This is the forest primeval. The murmuring pines and
    the hemlocks
Bearded with moss, and in garments green, indistinct in
    the twilight,
Stand like Druids of eld, with voices sad and prophetic,
Stand like harpies hoar, with beards that rest on their
    bosoms.
Loud from its rocky caverns, the deep-voiced neighboring
    ocean
Speaks, and in accents disconsolate answers the neighboring
    forest.

> [*Henry Wadsworth Longfellow*, Evangeline, *1847*]

ACROSTIC p. 37

M arble, weep, for thou dost cover
A dead beauty underneath thee,
R ich, as nature could bequeath thee:
G rant then, no rude hand remove her.
A ll the gazers on the skies
R ead not in fair heaven's story,
E xpresser truth, or truer glory,
T han they might, in her bright eyes.
R are, as wonder was her wit;
A nd, like Nectar ever flowing:
T ill time, strong by her bestowing,
C onquered hath both life and it.
L ife, whose grief was out of fashion,
I n these times. So few hath rued

F ate, in a brother. To conclude,
F or wit, feature, and true passion,
E arth, thou hast not such another.
                                [*Ben Jonson, "On Margaret Ratcliffe," 1616*]

ALCAIC STANZA p. 36

O mighty-mouthed inventor of harmonies,
O skilled to sing of Time or Eternity,
    God-gifted organ-voice of England,
        Milton, a name to resound for ages.
                                [*Lord Alfred Tennyson, "Milton," 1863*]

ALEXANDRINES UNRHYMED p. 11

"O," think I had I wings like to the simple dove,
This peril might I flye, and seek some place of rest
In wilder woods, where I might dwell far from these
        cares."
What speedy way of wing my plaints should they lay on,
To scape the stormy blast that threatened is to me!
                                [*Earl of Surrey, "Psalm Fifty-five," ca. 1545*]

ALEXANDRINES IN COUPLETS p. 11

Of Albion's glorious Isle the wonders whilst I write
The sundry varying soils, the pleasures infinite
(Where heat kills not the cold, nor cold expels the
        heat,
The alms too mildly small, nor winds too roughly great,
Nor night doth hinder day, nor day the night doth wrong,
The summer not too short, the winter not too long)
What help should I invoke to aid my Muse the while?
    Thou Genius of the place (this most renownèd Isle)
Which livedst long before the all-earth-drowning Flood,
Whilst yet the world did swarm with her gigantic brood;
Go thou before me still thy circling shores about
And in this wandering maze help to conduct me out.
                                [*Michael Drayton*, Poly-Olbion, *1613*]

ANACOLOUTHON p. 48

He listens in assurance, has no glance
To spare for them, but looks past steadily
At—at—
    A man's look completes itself.
       [Randall Jarrell, "The Knight, Death, and the Devil," 1955]

ANAPESTIC TETRAMETER p. 15

[See under Couplets, below]

ANAPESTS IN TRIMETER p. 15

Which I wish to remark,
And my language is plain
       [Bret Harte, "Plain Language from Truthful James," 1870]

ANAPESTS IN EIGHT FEET (IN THIS CASE
RIDICULOUSLY ALLITERATED)

From the depth of the dreamy decline of the dawn through
    a notable nimbus of nebulous noonshine,
Pallid and pink as the palm of the flag-flower that
    flickers with fear of the flies as they float
    [Algernon Charles Swinburne, "Nephelidia" (a self-parody), 1880]

ANAPHORA p. 48

And the pleasant water-courses,
You could trace them through the valley,
By the rushing in the Spring-time,
By the alders in the Summer,
By the white fog in the Autumn,
By the black line in the Winter . . .

    "I have given you lands to hunt in
I have given you streams to fish in,

I have given you bear and bison,
I have given you roe and reindeer,
I have given you brant and beaver . . ."
        [Henry Wadsworth Longfellow, The Song of Hiawatha, *1855]*

ANOMALOUS RHYME [1] p. 55

It's no go the picture palace, it's no go the stadium,
It's no go the country cot with a pot of pink geraniums,
It's no go the government grants, it's no go the elections,
Sit on your arse for fifty years and hang your hat on a pension.
        [Louis Macneice, "Bagpipe Music," 1937]

ANOMALOUS RHYME [2] p. 56

I grow old under an intensity
Of questioning looks. *Nonsense,*
I try to say, *I cannot teach you children*
How to live.—*If not you, who will?*
Cries one of them aloud, grasping my gilded
Frame till the world sways. *If not you, who will?*
        [James Merrill, "Mirror," 1959]

ANOMALOUS RHYME [3] SLANT *RIME RICHE*

I am the enemy you killed, my friend.
I knew you in the dark: for so you frowned
Yesterday through me as you jabbed and killed.
I parried, but my hands were loath and cold.
        [Wilfred Owen, "Strange Meeting," 1920]

APOSTROPHE p. 48

Bright Star, were I as steadfast as thou art
        [John Keats, Sonnet, 1819]

O wild West Wind, thou breath of Autumn's being
        [Percy Bysshe Shelley, "Ode to the West Wind," 1820]

BALLADE p. 42

Where are the holy apostles gone,
    Alb-clad and amice-tired and stoled
With the sacred tippet and that alone
    Wherewith, when he waxeth overbold,
    The foul fiend's throttle they take and hold?
All must come to the self-same bay;
    Sons and servants, their days are told:
The wind carries their like away.

Where is he now that held the throne
    Of Constantine with the hands of gold?
And the King of France, o'er all kings known
    For grace and worship that was extolled,
    Who convents and churches manifold
Built for God's service? In their day
    What of the honour they had? Behold,
The wind carries their like away.

Where are the champions every one,
    The Dauphins, the counsellors young and old?
The barons of Salins, Däl, Dijon,
    Vienne, Grenoble? They all are cold
    Or take the folk under their banner enrolled,—
Pursuivants, trumpeters, heralds, (hey!
    How they fed of the fat and the flagon trolled!)
The wind carries their like away.

[Envoy]
Princes to death are all foretold,
    Even as the humblest of their array:
Whether they sorrow, or whether they scold,
    The wind carries their like away.

           [*François Villon, "Ballad of Old-Time Lords,"*
           ca. 1460, translated by John Payne, 1900]

Where are the passions they essayed,
And where are the tears they made to flow?
Where the wild humors they portrayed
For laughing worlds to see and know?

Othello's wrath and Juliet's woe?
Sir Peter's whims and Timon's gall?
And Millamant and Romeo?
Into the night go one and all.

Where are the braveries, fresh or frayed?
The plumes, the armours—friend and foe?
The cloth of gold, the rare brocade,
The mantles glittering to and fro?
The pomp, the pride, the royal show?
The cries of war and festival?
The youth, the grace, the charm, the glow?
Into the night go one and all.

The curtain falls, the play is played,
The Beggar packs beside the Beau;
The Monarch troops, and troops the Maid,;
The Thunder huddles with the Snow.
Where are the revellers high and low?
The clashing swords? The lover's call?
The dancers gleaming row on row?
Into the night go one and all.

[Envoy]
Prince, in one common overthrow
The Hero tumbles with the Thrall:
As dust that drives, as straws that blow,
Into the night go one and all.

> *[William Ernest Henley, "Ballade of Dead Actors," 1888]*

BLANK VERSE pp. 12–13

From Tenedon, behold, in circles great
By the calm sea come fleeting adders twain
Which plièd toward the shore (I lothe to tell)
With rerèd breast lift up above the seas,
Whose bloody crests aloft the waves were seen.
Their hinder part swam hidden in the flood.
Their grisly back were linkèd manifold.

> *[Earl of Surrey, Virgil's Aeneid, II, ca. 1540]*

Was this the face that launched a thousand ships
And burnt the topless towers of Ilium?
Sweet Helen, make me immortal with a kiss:
Her lips suck forth my soul, see where it flies.
Come, Helen, come, give me my soul again.
Here will I dwell, for heaven is in these lips,
And all is dross that is not Helena.

[Christopher Marlowe, Doctor Faustus, 1604]

Yet not rejoicing in his speed, though bold,
Far off and fearless, nor with cause to boast,
Begins his dire attempt, which nigh the birth
Now rolling, boils in his tumultuous breast,
And like a devilish engine back recoils
Upon himself; horror and doubt distract
His troubled thoughts, and from the bottom stir
The hell within him, for within him hell
He brings, and round about him, nor from hell
One step no more than from himself can fly
By change of place . . .

[John Milton, Paradise Lost, 1667]

Or, where the Northern Ocean in vast whirls
Boils round the naked melancholy isles
Of farthest Thule, and the Atlantic surge
Pours in among the stormy Hebrides,
Who can recount what transmigrations there
Are annual made? what nations come and go?
And how the living clouds on clouds arise,
Infinite wings! till all the plume-dark air
And rude, resounding shore are one wild cry?

[James Thomson, Autumn, 1730]

Through Pope's soft song though all the Graces breathe,
And happiest art adorn his Attic page;
Yet does my mind with sweeter transport glow,
As at the spot of mossy trunk reclined,
In magic Spenser's softly-warbled song
I see deserted Una wander wide
Through wasteful solitudes, and lurid heaths . . .

[Thomas Warton, Jr., The Pleasures of Melancholy, 1745]

Forcing my way I came to one dear nook
Unvisited, where not a broken bough
Drooped with its withered leaves, ungracious sign
Of devastation; but the hazels rose
Tall and erect, with tempting clusters hung,
A virgin scene!—A little while I stood,
Breathing with such suppression of the heart
As joy delights in; and with wise restraint
Voluptuous, fearful of a rival, eyed
The banquet;—or beneath the trees I sate
Among the flowers, and with flowers I played.
                    [*William Wordsworth, "Nutting," 1798*]

For now the noonday quiet holds the hill:
The grasshopper is silent in the grass:
The lizard, with his shadow on the stone,
Rests like a shadow, and the winds are dead.
The purple flower droops: the golden bee
Is lily-cradled: I alone awake.
                    [*Lord Alfred Tennyson, "Oenone," 1832*]

We are upon the road. The thin swift moon
Runs with the running clouds that are the sky,
And with the running water runs, at whiles
Weak 'neath the film and heavy growth of reeds.
The country swims with motion. Time itself
Is consciously beside us, and perceived.
Our speed is such the sparks the engine leaves
Are burning after the whole train has passed.
The darkness is a tumult. We tear on,
The roll behind us and the cry before,
Constantly, in a roll of intense speed
And thunder. Any other sound is known
Merely by sight. The shrubs, the trees your eye
Scans for their growth, are far along in haze.
          [*Dante Gabriel Rossetti, "A Trip to Paris and Belgium," 1849*]

BLUES p. 45

I hate to see de evenin' sun go down,

Hate to see, de evenin' sun go down,
'Cause my baby, he done lef' dis town.

Feelin' tomorrow like I feel today
Feel tomorrow, like I feel today
I'll pack my trunk, make my getaway . . .
                    [*W. C. Handy, from "St. Louis Blues," 1914*]

CANZONE I pp. 59–60

The calm after a storm brought out the stars.
Glowworms signalling up from the sopping grass, no matter
That shutters of rain had opened over them, were also stars
Reflected upon. But constellations abound—those stars
Cut in my old tin lantern that hangs these nights
By the back door, electrified with curiosity. The stars
It throws along the granite stoop are no less true stars
For being poor man-mades. Last night they drew nothing
At first. Then, a luna moth, who battered at nothing,
The window of a theme, each pane a star
Whose frame I'd opened on the fluorescence in the day-
Light tube over the stove left on for her. Come day,

The greasy copper colander that shines for us by day
Was no more moon but a sweet gum grove, the stars
Of her submarginal eyelet spots blind to the day
I'd stumbled down on. The problem: what to do today
With her, a washed-out beauty that lingers, like the Matter
Of Rome? The old chroniclers, in their day,
Knew that history was for "writing up." What each day
Dealt was blocked out on the wiped slate of that night's
Sky. Then the stories from Freud's couch set the mind's
        night—
Life on his ear, until those star-studded myths saw day
Again—as when at the Lido a horse conjured out of nothing
Plunges through spotlights into a tank of women wearing
        nothing

But spangled belts. I was fifteen. "Oh, it's nothing,"

My mother said, when I asked why she'd winced. "The day,
The whole day's been tiring." At that age, there is nothing
To disbelieve. Now I realize she was right. It *was* nothing,
A flying horse, four girls who wanted next year to be stars
Somewhere else. Even the program (my French was up to
    nothing
More) spoke of *"aspirations des artistes."* There seemed
    nothing
That first trip abroad, that didn't hum with "What's the
    matter?"
The hereditary instructions written down in every bit of
    matter
Might as well have read *Mind* and *Eat It All* and *Touch Nothing*,
Each nucleotide a stern look that *Might Have Consequences
    Tonight.*
And after that show, they did. No sooner in bed by midnight,

I had sneaked out of the hotel, determined only at night
Would any City of Light appear. I found next to nothing
From my Guide Noir. Cafés touted as *"les gares de la nuit"*
Were a wood of murmuring cognac leaves too soon ignited
By a deep inhale. The pissoir's perforated necessity (that day
I had slipped in one and been scolded) was, overnight,
Changed into an iron fruit heady with poisons, like night-
Shade. How did I not lose myself? Down three-star
Back ways, over floodlit bridges, guided by those stars
That steered toward now, hours later—as long as last night—
I woke the sleeping doorman with a yawn. Then, the matter
Of facing *her.* But—she hadn't noticed. There was the matter

Too of luggage to count, plane to catch, the papal diplomat her
Mother knew. . . . One apple-green case waits to be reunited
With the rest. The luna moth. I let her go. A matter
Of endangered species. Sunstruck, wobbly, a smattering
Of inflected throbs, she started underground. Nothing
I could urge made her fly up, fly home. What matter
Where I fly, she seemed to say, beating against the matted
Cloverleaf. There was no point but to watch as the day's
Earliest cock robin caught on, instinct's idée
Fixe. Worried by the wingspan and so the madder

For it, he made his dive for her. Head to head, the star-
Crossed pair shuddered in violent agreement. Now there
    stares

Back at me from a wet paving stone the envoy of someday
In my past, half a wing and its teardop tail, nothing
So much as a scrap with its scribbled message *"Tonight."*
I'm reminded to look back, back through whatever the matter
Was, and see what's left over. It might as well be stars.
                        [*J. D. McClatchy, "The Luna Moth," 1986*]

CANZONE II p. 61

A bright jewelled beetle like a clump of fire
Glowed at her throat as the sun went rolling out
Over my shoulder, while an incredible
Dark colony of garnets crowning her wrist
Fell, as the deck heaved under us, to shaking.
Our hands touched. The bug blew in the wind and clung,
As if hanged by the nap of the wool she wore.

Could I have found a better jewel to buy her
Than such an insect, it might have made a shout
Of its shining with every crystal syllable
To intimate such farewells from her breast
As if to feign a sorrier forsaking
Than our impermanent parting, as she hung,
Clasped clinging to my neck, and cried and swore.

No lapidary joy of gold and wire
Clasped both our brows so intricately about,
But no mere sea-grief swelled her eyes so full
When I, uneasy lepidopterist,
Made light of the bug; when, as if by my making,
Five crystal tears splashed down her arm among
The garnets, and made them seem pismires all the more.

Their antic sparkling composed our speech entire:
Salt tears flashed within the stones. The sea without
Echoed our silence, till one shrieking gull

Stooped, of a sudden, as if at an amethyst
In the head of the beetle, and all its undertaking
Seemed aimed at that ontic bug; then the bird slung
Its body and its being toward the shore.

O Bug bug bug bug bug that did require
The quietest devotions of our doubt!
At once a lump of crafted mineral,
Whose crystals no reflection could resist,
And a real beetle, whose safety lay in faking
The fixity of jewels, lest some toxin-tongue
Enjoy its Janus facets to the core.

Just then the wind blew up a little higher,
Inflaming the sunset until there was no doubt
But that departure was upon us; still,
The whistle, the irritant bell, had to insist
That the giving of gifts was done, but for our breaking:
A venomous tocsin rolled; when it had rung,
A swarm of June bees drew up in a roar.

No longer then could she and I conspire
About the bug, all bustling and devout,
To make our delaying less discernible.
A pair of antiquarians, we kissed
And clipped, then parted, querulous and quaking.
I wished her joy of the bug, at which she flung
Her jewels to the sea, to spawn upon its floor.

> While in my hand remained five bright tears, wrung
> Like tiny insects of sweat from every pore.
> *[John Hollander, "Canzona: A Parting on Shipboard," 1952]*

CAROL pp. 37–38

Evermore, wheresoever I be
The dread of death doth trouble me.

As I went me for to solàce
I heard a man sigh and say "Alas!

Of me now thus standeth the case:
The dread of death doth trouble me.

I have been lord of tower and town
I set nought by my great renown,
For death will pluck it all a-down:
The dread of death doth trouble me.

When I shall die I am not sure,
In what country or in what hour;
Wherefor I sobbing say to my power,
'The dread of death doth trouble me' . . ." etc.
                    [Anonymous, untitled, ca. 1470 (text modernized)]

CHIASMUS p. 49

With mourning pine I; you with pining mourn.
                    [Edmund Spenser, "January," 1579]

These flowery waters and these watery flowers
                    [Robert Frost, "Spring Pools," 1928]

In Xanadu did Kubla Khan
                    [Samuel Taylor Coleridge, "Kubla Khan," 1797]

And your quaint honor turn to dust
And into ashes, all my lust.
                    [Andrew Marvell, "To His Coy Mistress," 1680]

A fop their passion, but their prize, a sot
                    [Alexander Pope, "Epistle to a Lady," 1735]

CLERIHEW p. 46

E. C. Bentley
Told a friend, very gently,
"When you die, and they bury you,
I'll preserve your name in a clerihew."
                    [John Hollander, "Bentley," 1999]

COUPLETS OF PENTAMETER AND
TETRAMETER pp. 15, 58

Till we have flourished, grown, and reaped our wishes
    What conscience dares oppose our kisses?
But when time's colder hand leads us near home,
    Then let that winter-virtue come:
Frost is till then prodigious: we may do
    What youth and pleasure prompts us to.
                    [Thomas Randolph, "Upon Love Fondly
                           Refused for Conscience's Sake," 1638]

Tetrameter couplets p. 15

While thus he threw his elbow round,
Depopulating all the ground,
And, with his whistling scythe, does cut
Each stroke between the earth and root,
The edgèd steel by careless chance
Did into his own ankle glance;
And there among the grass fell down,
By his own scythe, the mower mown.
                [Andrew Marvell, "Damon the Mower," 1681]

Anapestic tetrameter couplets pp. 15–16
(here in staves of four lines)

(Elegiac mode)
The blackbird has fled to another retreat,
Where the hazels afford him a screen from the heat,
And the scene where his melody charm'd me before
Resounds with his sweet flowing ditty no more.
                [William Cowper, "The Poplar Field," 1791]

(Bouncy mode)
The Assyrian came down like the wolf on the fold
And his cohorts were gleaming in purple and gold;
And the sheen of their spears was like stars on the sea,
When the blue waves rolls nightly on deep Galilee.
        [Lord Byron, "The Destruction of Sennacherib," 1815]

DACTYLS IN EIGHT FEET p. 8

As for Venice and her people, merely born to bloom
     and drop,
Here on earth they bore their fruitage, mirth and
     folly were the crop:
What of soul was left, I wonder, when the kissing
     had to stop?

                    [*Robert Browning, "A Toccata of Galuppi's," 1847*)

Many a night from yonder ivied casement, ere I went to
     rest,
Did I look on great Orion sloping slowly to the west.

Many a night I saw the Pleaids, rising through the mellow
     shade,
Glitter like a swarm of fire-flies tangled in a silver braid.
                    •   •   •

In the spring a livelier iris changes on the burnished
     dove,
In the spring a young man's fancy lightly turns to
     thoughts of love.

                    [*Lord Alfred Tennyson, "Locksley Hall," 1842*]

ECHO POEM p. 37

O who will show me those delights on high?
Echo.   I.
Thou Echo, thou art mortal, all men know.
Echo.   No.
Wert thou not born among the trees and leaves?
Echo.   Leaves.
And are there any leaves, that still abide?
Echo.   Bide.
What leaves are they? impart the matter wholly.
Echo.   Holy.
Are holy leaves the Echo then of bliss?
Echo.   Yes.
Then tell me, what is the supreme delight?
Echo.   Light.

Light to the mind: what shall the will enjoy?
Echo.   Joy.
But are there cares and business with the pleasure?
Echo.   Leisure.
Light, joy, and leisure; but shall they persever?
Echo.   Ever.

[George Herbert, "Heaven," 1633]

ELEGIAC COUPLETS (ACCENTUAL) p. 36

Never regret it, my love, that you gave yourself to me so
    quickly!
    Know that I never could think anything shameful of you.
Cupid's arrows work so very variously, some merely graze us,
    But then their poison afflicts our suffering hearts for
    years.
Others, with freshly sharpened points, though, and heavier
    feathers
    Pierce us through to the quick, and swiftly ignite our
    blood.

[J. W. von Goethe, from "Roman Elegies"
(1795), translated by John Hollander]

EPIC SIMILE p. 48

[Athena diverts Pandarus' arrow from Menelaus:]
She brushed it away from his skin as lightly as when a mother
brushes a fly away from her child who is lying in sweet sleep.
    [Homer, Iliad, *translated by Richmond Lattimore, 1951]*

[The noise of battle at one point in the Trojan War]
Earth flow'd with blood. And, as from hills, rain waters
    headlong fall
That always eat huge ruts which, met in one bed, fill a vall
With such a confluence of streams that on the mountain
    grounds
Far off, in frighted shepherds' ears the bustling noise
    rebounds:
So grew their conflicts, and so showed their scuffling to the
    ear

With flight and clamor still commixed, and all effects of
fear.
[Homer, Iliad, translated by George Chapman, 1611]

"EPODE COUPLETS" p. 58

Luxurious man, to bring his vice to use,
   Did after him the world seduce,
And from the fields where flowers and plants allure,
   Where nature was most plain and pure.
[Andrew Marvell, "The Mower Against Gardens," 1681]

EUGENE ONEGIN STANZA p. 58

Our hero to the doors is driven
And darting up the marble stair
Straight past the porter, having given
The final smoothing to his hair,
Enters the hall. The crowd has thickened,
The band of its own din has sickened.
On the mazurka now intent
In circling buzz the mob is pent,
And the horse-guardsmen's spurs are clashing.
Swift scurry the dear ladies' feet;
After those charming footsteps fleet
How many a fiery glance is flashing!
The fiddle's squeal the murmuring drowns
Of jealous dames in modish gowns.
[Alexander Pushkin, Eugene Onegin,
translated by Oliver Elton, 1934]

FOURTEENERS IN COUPLETS p. 11

And as she ran the meeting windes hir garments backward
   blue
So that hir naked skinne apearde behind hir as she flue,
Hir goodly yellow golden haire that hangèd loose and slacke,
With every puffe of ayre did wave and tosse behind her back.
Hir running made hir seeme more fayre, the youthfull God

therefore
Could not abide to waste his wordes in dalyance any more.
[*Ovid*, Metamorphoses, *translated by Arthur Golding, 1567*]

Achilles' banefull wrath resound, O Goddesse, that imposd
Infinite sorrowes on the Greekes, and many brave souls losd
From breasts Heroique—sent them farre, to that invisible
cave
That no light comforts; and their lims to dogs and vultures
gave.
To all which Jove's will gave effect; from whom first strife
begunne
Betwixt Atrides, king of men, and Thetis' godlike Sonne.
[*Homer*, Iliad, *translated by George Chapman, 1611*]

Unrhymed fourteeners p. 11

With what sense is it that the chicken shuns the ravenous
hawk?
With what sense does the tame pigeon measure out the
expanse?
With what sense does the bee form cells? have not the mouse
& frog
Eyes and ears and sense of touch? yet are their habitations
And their pursuits as different as their forms and as their
joys . . .
[*William Blake*, Visions of the Daughters of Albion, *1793*]

FREE VERSE pp. 26–30

Hebrew Bible in King James Version

1. The heavens declare the glory of God, and the firmament
   sheweth his handywork.
2. Day unto day uttereth speech, and night unto night sheweth
   knowledge.
3. There is no speech nor language whether their voice is not
   heard.
4. Their line is gone out through all the earth, and their words
   to the end of the world. In them hath he set a tabernacle
   for the sun,

5. Which is as a bridegroom coming out of his chamber, and
    rejoiceth as a strong man to run a race.

                                               [King James Version, Psalm 19, 1602]

End-stopped

When the white dawn first
Through the rough fir-planks
Of my hut, by the chestnuts,
Up at the valley-head,
Came breaking, Goddess!
I sprang up, threw around me
My dappled fawn-skin;
Passing out, from the wet turf
Where they lay, by the hut door,
I snatched up my vine-crown, my fir-staff,
All drenched in dew—

                       [Matthew Arnold, "The Strayed Reveller," 1849]

I heard you solemn-sweet pipes of the organ as last Sunday
    morn I pass'd the church,
Winds of autumn, as I walk'd the woods at dusk I heard
    your long-stretch'd sighs above so mournful,
I heard the perfect Italian tenor singing at the opera, I
    heard the soprano in the midst of the quartet singing;
Heart of my love! you too I heard murmuring low through
    one of the wrists around my head,
Heard the pulse of you when all was still ringing little bells
    last night under my ear.

               [Walt Whitman, "I Heard You . . . etc.," 1861]

Enjambed

for I went spinning on the

four wheels of my car
along the wet road until

I saw a girl with one leg
over the rail of a balcony

         [William Carlos Williams, "The Right of Way," 1923]

GHAZAL p. 66

To this khan, and from this khan
    How many pilgrims came and went too!
In this khan, and by this khan
    What arts were spent, what hearts were rent too!
To this khan and from this khan
    (Which, for penance, man is sent to)
Many a van and caravan
    Crowded came, and shrouded went too.
Christian man and Mussulman,
    Guebre, heathen, Jew, and Gentoo,
To this khan, and from this khan,
    Weeping came, and sleeping went too.
A riddle this since time began,
    Which many a sage his mind hath bent to:
All came, all went; but never man
    Knew whence they came, or where they went to!
                    [*James Clarence Mangan, "Ghazel: The World," 1838*]

HENDECASYLLABICS p. 36

Till I heard as it were a noise of waters
Moving tremulous under feet of angels
Multitudinous, out of all the heavens;
Knew the fluttering wind, the fluttered foliage,
Shakes fitfully, full of sound and shadow . . .
                    [*A. C. Swinburne, "Hendecasyllabics," 1866*]

HEROIC COUPLETS pp. 14–15

End-stopped

Thames, the most lov'd of all the Ocean's sons,
By his old sire to his embraces runs,
Hasting to pay his tribute to the Sea,
Like mortal life to meet Eternity . . .
Finds wealth where 'tis, bestows it where it wants,
Cities in deserts, woods in Cities plants,
So that to us, no thing, no place is strange

While his fair bosom is the world's exchange.
O could I flow like thee, and make thy stream
My great example, as it is my theme!
Though deep, yet clear, though gentle, yet not dull,
Strong without rage, without o'erflowing, full.
                              [Sir John Denham, Cooper's Hill, *1642]*

Enjambed

.... Sir, 'twas not
Her husband's presence only, called that spot
Of joy into the Duchess' cheek: perhaps
Frà Pandolf chanced to say, "Her mantle laps
Over my lady's wrist too much," or "Paint
Must never hope to reproduce the faint
Half-flush that dies along her throat:" such stuff
Was courtesy, she thought, and cause enough
For calling up that spot of joy. . . .
                      [Robert Browning, "My Last Duchess," 1842]

HEXAMETERS, MASCULINE ENDING,
IN RHYMED STANZAS p. 36

Well, it is earth with me; silence resumes her reign:
    I will be patient and proud, and soberly acquiesce.
Give me the keys. I feel for the common chord again,
    Sliding by semitone, till I sink to the minor—yes,
And I blunt it into a ninth, and I stand on alien ground,
    Surveying awhile the heights I rolled from into the
        deep;
Which, hark, I have dared and done, for my resting-
        place is found
The C Major of this life: so now I will try to sleep.
                          [Robert Browning, "Abt Vogler," 1864]

IAMBS

In trimeter

There was a naughty boy
A naughty boy was he
                  [John Keats, "A Song about Myself," 1818]

In tetrameter

The grave's a fine and private place
But none I think do there embrace.

[Andrew Marvell, "The Garden," 1681]

In pentameter

The curfew tolls the knell of parting day,
The lowing herd winds slowly o'er the lea

[Thomas Gray, "Elegy in a Country Churchyard," 1751]

INTERNAL RHYME p. 64

Therefore now I abide for a season in silence. I know
I shall die as my fathers died, and sleep as they sleep; even
so.
For the glass of the years is brittle wherein we gaze for a
span;
A little soul for a little bears up this corpse which is man.
So long I endure; no longer; and laugh not again, neither
weep.
For there is no God found stronger than death; and death is a
sleep.

[Algernon Charles Swinburne, "Hymn to Proserpine," 1866]

LIMERICK p. 46

There was a Young Lady of Lucca
Whose lovers completely forsook her;
   She ran up a tree,
   And said "Fiddle-dee-dee!"
Which embarrassed the people of Lucca.

[Edward Lear, 1845]

ODE: CLASSICAL TRIAD pp. 33–34

[The Turne]
Brave Infant of *Saguntum*, cleare
Thy comming forth in that great yeare,

When the Prodigious *Hannibal* did crowne
His rage, with razing your immortall Towne.
Thou, looking then about,
E're thou wert halfe got out,
Wise child, did'st hastily returne,
And mad'st thy Mothers wombe thine urne.
How summ'd a circle didst thou leave man-kind
Of deepest lore, could we the Center find!

[The Counter-Turne]
Did wiser nature draw thee back,
From out the horrour of that sack,
Where shame, faith, honour, and regard of right
Lay trampled on; the deeds of death, and night,
Urg'd, hurried forth, and horld
Upon th'affrighted world:
Sword, fire, and famine, with fell fury met;
And all on utmost ruine set;
As, could they but lifes miseries fore-see,
No doubt all Infants would returne like thee?

[The Stand]
For, what is life, if measured by the space,
Not by the act?
Or masked man, if valu'd by his face,
Above his fact?
Here's one out-lived his Peeres,
And told forth fourescore yeares;
He vexed time, and busied the whole State;
Troubled both foes, and friends;
But ever to no ends:
What did this Stirrer, but die late?
How well at twentie had he falne, or stood!
For three of his foure-score, he did no good.
  [Ben Jonson, from "To the Immortall Memorie, and Friendship of
    That Noble Paire, Sir Lucius Cary, and Sir H. Morison," 1640]

PANTOUM (FIRST FIVE STANZAS) p. 44

The wind brings up the hawthorn's breath,
The sweet airs ripple up the lake:

My soul, my soul is sick to death,
My heart, my heart is like to break.

The sweet airs ripple up the lake,
I hear the thin woods' fluttering:
My heart, my heart is like to break;
What part have I, alas, in spring?

I hear the thin woods' fluttering:
The brake is brimmed with linnet-song:
What part have I, alas, in spring?
For me, hearts' winter is lifelong.

The brake is brimmed with linnet-song;
Clear carols flutter through the trees
For me, hearts' winter is lifelong;
I cast my sighs on every breeze . . .

                                        [John Payne, "Pantoum," 1884]

PATTERN POEM p. 31

          A broken ALTAR, Lord, thy servant rears
          Made of a heart, and cemented with tears
              Whose parts are as thy hand did frame
              No workman's tool hath touched the same
                          A   HEART   alone
                          Is   such   a   stone
                          As   nothing   but
                          Thy pow'r doth cut.
                          Wherefore each part
                          Of my hard heart
                          Meets in thy frame
                          To praise thy Name:
              That, if I chance to hold my peace,
              These stones to praise thee may not cease.
          O let thy blessed SACRIFICE be mine
          And sanctify this ALTAR to be thine.
                              [George Herbert, "The Altar," 1635]

POP STANDARD, *AABA* pp. 45–46

(verse)
They call you Lady Luck
But there is room for doubt
At times you have a most unLadylike way of running
    out
You're on this date with me
The pickings have been lush
And yet before this evening is over
You might give me the brush
You might forget your manners
You might refuse to stay and so
The best that I can do is pray

(chorus)
Luck, be a lady tonght
Luck, be a lady tonight
Luck, if you've ever been a lady to begin with
Luck, be a lady tonight.

Luck, let a gentleman see
How nice a dame you can be
I know the way you've treated other guys you've been
    with
Luck, be a lady with me.

A lady doesn't leave her escort
It isn't fair, it isn't nice
A lady doesn't wander all over the room
And blow on some other guy's dice

So let's keep the party polite
Never get out of my sight
Stick with me, baby, I'm the fellow you came in with
Luck, be a lady
Luck, be a lady
Luck, be a lady tonight.
        [Frank Loesser, "Luck, Be a Lady," from Guys and Dolls, *1950]*

POULTERS' MEASURE p. 11

To water sundry seeds, the furrow by the way
A running river, trilling down with liquor, can convey.
    Behold, with lively hue fair flow'rs that shine so bright;
With riches, like the orient gems, they paint the old in sight.
    Bees, humming with soft sound (their murmur is so small),
Of blooms and blossoms suck the tops; on dewèd leaves they
    fall.
    The creeping vine holds down her own bewedded elms,
And, wandering out with branches thick, reeds folded
    overwhelms.
                                  [*Nicholas Grimald, "The Garden," 1557*]

ELIZABETHAN "QUANTITATIVE" HEXAMETERS p. 35

Then, lo ye, from Tenedos through standing deep flood
    appeasèd
—I shiver in telling—two serpents, monsterous, ugly
Plash'd the water sulking, to the shore most hastily swinging;
Whose breasts upsteaming and manes blood-speckled
    enhanced
High the sea surmounted; the rest in smooth flood is hidden.
                                  [*Richard Stanyhurst,* The First Four
                                  Books of Virgil His Aeneas, *1582*]

RONDEAU p. 43

Death, of thee do I make my moan,
    Who hadst my lady away from me,
    Nor wilt assuage thine enmity
Till with her life thou hast mine own;
For since that hour my strength has flown.
    Lo! what wrong was her life to thee,
                Death?

Two we were, and the heart was one;
   Which now being dead, I dead must be,
   Or seem alive so lifelessly
As in the choir the painted stone,
            Death!
                  [François Villon, "To Death, of His Lady,"
                    translated by Dante Gabriel Rossetti, 1869]

In Flanders Fields the poppies blow
Between the crosses, row on row,
   That mark out place, and in the sky
   The larks, still bravely singing, fly
Scarce heard amid the guns below.

We are the Dead. Short time ago
We lived, felt dawn, saw sunset glow,
   Loved and were loved, and now we lie
          In Flanders fields.

Take up our quarrel with the foe:
To you from failing hands we throw
   The torch; be yours to hold it high.
   If ye break faith with us who die
We shall not sleep, though poppies grow
          In Flanders fields.
                [John McCrae, "In Flanders Fields," 1918]

RONDEAU REDOUBLÉ p. 63

My day and night are in my lady's hand;
I have no other sunrise than her sight;
   For me her favour glorifies the land;
Her anger darkens all the cheerful light.

   Her face is fairer than the hawthorn white,
When all a-flower in May the hedgerows stand;
   While she is kind, I know of no affright;
My day and night are in my lady's hand.

   All heaven in her glorious eye is spanned;
Her smile is softer than the summer's night,

Gladder than daybreak on the Faery strand;
I have no other sunrise than her sight.

Her silver speech is like the singing flight
Of runnels rippling o'er the jewelled sand;
Her kiss a dream of delicate delight;
For me her favour glorifies the land.

What if the Winter chase the Summer bland!
The gold sun in her hair burns ever bright.
If she be sad, straightway all joy is banned;
Her anger darkens all the cheerful light.

Come weal or woe, I am my lady's knight
And in her service every ill withstand;
Love is my Lord in al the world's despite
And holdeth in the hollow of his hand
                    My day and night.
              [*John Payne, "Rondeau Redoublé," 1880*]

RONDEL p. 62

The wind's way in the deep sky's hollow
None may measure, as none can say
How the heart in her shows the swallow
    The wind's way.

Hope nor fear can avail to stay
Waves that whiten on wrecks that wallow,
Times and seasons that wane and slay.

Life and love, till the strong night swallow
Thought and hope and the red last ray,
Swim the waters of years that follow
    The wind's way.
        [*Algernon Charles Swinburne, "The Way of the Wind," 1883*]

SESTINA pp. 40–41

To the dim light and the large circle of shade
I have clomb, and to the whitening of the hills,

There where we see no colour in the grass.
Nathless my longing loses not its green,
It has so taken root in the hard stone
Which talks and hears as though it were a lady.

Utterly frozen is this youthful lady,
Even as the snow that lies within the shade;
For she is no more moved than is the stone
By the sweet season which makes warm the hills
And alters them afresh from white to green,
Covering their sides again with flowers and grass.

When on her hair she sets a crown of grass
The thought has no more room for other lady;
Because she weaves the yellow with the green
So well that Love sits down there in the shade,—
Love who has shut me in among low hills
Faster than between walls of granite-stone.

She is no more bright than is a precious stone;
The wound she gives may not be healed with grass:
I therefore have fled far o'er plains and hills
For refuge from so dangerous a lady;
But from her sunshine nothing can give shade,—
Not any hill, nor wall, nor summer-green.

A while ago, I saw her dressed in green,—
So fair, she might have wakened in a stone
This love which I do feel even for her shade;
And therefore, as one woos a graceful lady,
I wooed her in a field that was all grass
Girdled about with very lofty hills.

Yet shall the streams turn back and climb the hills
Before Love's flame in this damp wood and green
Burn, as it burns within a youthful lady,
For my sake, who would sleep away in stone
My life, or feed like beasts upon the grass,
Only to see her garments cast a shade.

How dark so'er the hills throw out their shade,
Under her summer-green the beautiful lady

Covers it, like a stone covered in grass.
> [Dante Alighieri, "Sestina: Of the Lady Pietra degli Scrovigni,"
> translated by Dante Gabriel Rossetti, 1861]

SESTINA, RHYMED

I saw my soul at rest upon a day
  As a bird sleeping in the nest of night,
Among soft leaves that give the starlight way
  To touch its wings but not its eyes with light;
So that it knew as one in visions may,
  And knew not as men waking, of delight.

This was the measure of my soul's delight;
  It had no power of joy to fly by day,
Nor part in the large lordship of the light;
  But in the secret moon-beholden way
Had all its will of dreams and pleasant night,
  And all the love and life that sleepers may.

But such life's triumph as men waking may
  It might not have to feed its faint delight
Between the stars by night and sun by day,
  Shut up with green leaves and a little light;
Because its way was as a lost star's way,
  A world's not wholly known of day or night.

All loves and dreams and sounds and gleams of night
  Made it all music that such minstrels may,
And all they had they gave it of delight;
  But in the full face of the fire of day
What place shall be for any starry light,
  What part of heaven in all the wide sun's way?

Yet the soul woke not, sleeping by the way,
  Watched as a nursling of the large-eyed night,
And sought no strength nor knowledge of the day,
  Nor closer touch conclusive of delight,
Nor mightier joy nor truer than dreamers may,
  Nor more of song than they, nor more of light.

For who sleeps once sees the secret light
   Whereby sleep shows the soul a fairer way
Between the rise and rest of day and night,
   Shall care no more to fare as all men may,
But be his place of pain or of delight,
   There shall he dwell, beholding night as day.

Song, have thy day and take thy fill of light
   Before the night be fallen across the way;
Sing while he may, man hath no long delight.
                  [Algernon Charles Swinburne, "Sestina," 1878]

SKELTONICS pp. 22–23

Merry Margaret, as midsummer flower,
Gentle as falcon or hawk of the tower,
With solace and gladness,
Much mirth and no madness,
All good and no badness;
So joyously,
So maidenly,
So womanly,
Her demeaning:
In every thing
Far far passing
That I can indite
Or suffice to write
Of merry Margaret, as midsummer flower,
Gentle as falcon or hawk of the tower. . . .
          [John Skelton, "To Mistress Margaret Hussey," 1523]

SONNET pp. 19–21

Shakespearean

When to the sessions of sweet silent thought
I summon up remembrance of things past,
I sigh the lack of many a thing I sought,
And with old woes new wail my dear time's waste:
Then can I drown an eye, unused to flow
For precious friends hid in death's dateless night,

And weep afresh love's long since cancelled woe,
And moan the expense of many a vanished sight:
Then can I grieve at grievances foregone,
And heavily from woe to woe tell o'er
The sad account of fore-bemoanèd moan,
Which I new pay as if not paid before.
  But if the while I think on thee, dear friend,
  All losses are restored and sorrows end.
                          [William Shakespeare, Sonnet 30, 1609]

Italian

How soon hath Time, the subtle thief of youth
  Stolen on his wing my three-and-twentieth year!
  My hasting days fly on with full career,
  But my late spring no bud or blossom showeth.
Perhaps my semblance might deceive the truth
  That I to manhood am arrived so near,
  And inward ripeness doth much less appear,
  That some more timely-happy spirits endueth.
Yet it be less or more, or soon or slow,
  It shall be still in stricter measure even
  To that same lot, however mean or high,
Toward which time leads me, and thr will of heaven;
  All is, if I have grace to use it so,
  As ever in my great task-master's eye.
                          [John Milton, Sonnet 7, 1673]

Spenserian

Fresh spring, the herald of love's mighty king,
In whose coat armour richly are displayed
All sorts of flowers the which on earth do spring
  In goodly colours gloriously arrayed;
Go to my love, where she is careless laid,
Yet in her winter's bower not well awake;
  Tell her the joyous time will not be stayed
  Unless she do him by the forelock take.
Bid her therefore herself soon ready make,
  To wait on love amongst his lively crew;
  Where every one that misseth then her make   [mate]
  Shall be by him amerced with penance due.

Make haste therefore, sweet love, whilst it is prime,
    For none can call again the passèd time
                            [Edmund Spenser, Amoretti *70, 1594]*

Tailed sonnet

Because you have thrown off your Prelate Lord,
    And with stiff vows renounced his Liturgy,
    To seize the widowed whore Plurality
    From them whose sin ye envied, not abhorred,
Dare ye for this abjure the civil sword
    To force our consciences that Christ set free,
    And ride us with a Classic Hierarchy
    Taught ye by mere A. S. and Rutherford?
Men whose life, learning, faith and pure intent
    Would have been held in high esteem with Paul
    Must now be named and printed heretics
By shallow Edward and Scotch what dye call!
    But we do hope to find out all your tricks,
    Your plots and packing worse than those of Trent,
                That so the Parliament
May with their wholesome and preventive shears
Clip your phylacteries, though baulk your ears,
                 And succour our just fears
When they shall read this clearly in your charge,—
New *Presbyter* is but old *Priest* writ large.
               [John Milton, "On the New Forcers of Conscience
                        under the Long Parliament," 1647]

Meredithian sonnet

What are we first? First, animals; and next
Intelligences at a leap, on whom
Pale lies the distant shadow of the tomb,
And all that draweth on the tomb for text.
Into which state comes Love, the crowning sun:
Beneath whose light the shadow loses form.
We are the lords of life, and life is warm.
Intelligence and instinct now are one.
But nature says: "My children most they seem
When they least know me: therefore I decree
That they shall suffer." Swift doth young Love flee,

And we stand wakened, shivering from our dream.
Then if we study Nature we are wise.
Thus do the few who live but with the day:
The scientific animals are they.—
Lady, this my sonnet to your eyes.

[George Meredith, "Modern Love," 1861]

Blank sonnet p. 57

O thou whose face hath felt the winter's wind,
    Whose eye has seen the snow-clouds hung in mist,
    And thee black elm-tops 'mong the freezing stars,
    To thee the spring will be a harvest-time.
O thou, whose only book has been the light
    Of supreme darkness when thou feddest on
    Night after night when Phoebus was away,
    To thee the spring shall be a triple morn.
O, fret not after knowledge—I have none,
    And yet my song comes native with the warmth
O, fret not after knowledge—I have none,
    And yet the evening listens. He who saddens
At thought of idleness cannot be idle
And he's awake who thinks himself asleep.

[John Keats, untitled sonnet, 1818]

Thirteener

The low wind, the loud gulls and the bare, egregious cry
Of a goat somewhere around the point the land urges
On the unteachable bay: these have taken of late
To commenting on our two forms—differently placed,
Each observable only in quite another kind
Of light—posed silently, sombre-hearted among them.
What they say is as unfathomable as what we
See, gazing out between mildly distant islands at
A horizon contrived by gray sky and gray water.
The nearby green water, with no memory of all
That distant amplitude of sea, slaps playfully at
These contemplative rocks which might be ourselves but for
Our darkening power to behold them and compare.

[John Hollander, "Further Clarities," 1983]

SPRUNG RHYTHM (HERE, FIVE BEAT) p. 22

O the mind, mind has mountains; cliffs of fall
Frightful, sheer, no-man-fathomed. Hold them cheap
May who ne'er hung there. Nor does long our small
Durance deal with that steep or deep. Here! creep,
Wretch, under a comfort serves in a whirlwind: all
Life death does end and each day dies with sleep.
                    [G. M. Hopkins, "No Worst, There Is None," 1885]

STANZA FORMS pp. 16–19

Rhymed tercets p. 16

[tetrameter]
Enclose me still for fear I START;
Be to me rather sharp and TART,
Than let me want my hand and ART.

When thou dost greater judgments SPARE,
And with thy knife but prune and PARE,
Even fruitful trees more fruitful ARE.
                    [George Herbert, "Paradise," 1633]

[pentameter]
A little hearth best fits a little fire
A little chapel fits a little choir,
As my small bell best fits my little spire.

A little stream best fits a little boat;
A little lead best fits a little float;
As my small pipe best fits my little note
                    [Robert Herrick, "A Ternary of Littles, upon
                    a Pipkin of Jelly Sent to a Lady," 1648]

Quatrains of various sorts pp. 16–18

Ballad stanza p. 16

The wind doth blow today, my love,
    And a few small drops of rain;

I never had but one true-love,
   In cold grave she was lain.
            [Anonymous, "The Unquiet Grave," ca. 1500]

—and used outside of ballads themselves:
All dripping in tangles green,
   Cast up by a lone sea,
If purer for that, O Weed,
   Bitterer, too, are ye?

            [Herman Melville, "The Tuft of Kelp," 1888]

"Common measure" pp. 16–17

We hanged our harps and instruments
   the willow trees upon
For in that place men for their use
   had planted many one.
            [Psalm 137, versified by Sternhold and Hopkins, 1562]

Deep in unfathomable mines
   Of never-failing skill
He treasures up his bright designs
   And works his sovereign will.
            [William Cowper, "Light Shining out of Darkness," 1773]

An example from Emily Dickinson p. 17

Because I could not stop for Death,
   He kindly stopped for me;
The Carriage held but just ourselves
   And Immortality.
            [Emily Dickinson, untitled, ca. 1863]

"Long measure" p. 17

Hark! the cock proclaims the morning
   Match the rime, and strike the strings;
Heav'nly muse, embrace the warning,
   Raise thy voice, and stretch they wings.
            [Christopher Smart, "Hymn VIII," 1765]

—or, outside of hymnody, simply as a tetrameter, cross-
   rhymed quatrain:
It matters not how strait the gate
How charged with punishments the scroll
I am the master of my fate,
I am the captain of my soul
                            [William Ernest Henley, "Invictus," 1898]

—or, rhymed *aabb*
In contact, lo! the flint and steel,
By spark and flame, the thought reveal,
That he, the metal, she the stone
Had cherished secretly, alone.
                            [Ambrose Bierce, "Alone," 1906]

In Memoriam *stanza p. 16*

Now rings the woodland loud and long,
   The distance takes a livelier hue,
   And drowned in yonder living blue
The lark becomes a sightless song.
                            [Lord Alfred Tennyson, In Memoriam CXV, *1850]*

Though beauty be the mark of praise,
   And yours of whom I sing be such
   As not the world can praise too much
Yet is't your virtue now I raise.
                            [Ben Jonson, "An Elegy," 1640]

Rubaiyat *stanzas p. 16*

A Book of Verses, underneath the Bough,
A jug of Wine, a Loaf of Bread—and Thou
   Beside me singing in the Wilderness—
Oh, Wilderness were Paradise enow!
                            [Edward Fitzgerald, The Rubaiyat of Omar Khayyam, *1872]*

Night falls like fire; the heavy lights run low,
And as they drop, my blood and body so
   Shake as the flame shakes, full of days and hours
That sleep not neither weep they as they go . . .
                            [Algernon Charles Swinburne, "Laus Veneris," 1866]

—or, the same in tetrameter
How richly down the rocky dell
The torrent vineyard streaming fell
   To meet the sun and sunny waters,
That only heaved with summer swell.
                [Lord Alfred Tennyson, "The Daisy," 1907]

Sapphic stanza pp. 17–18

As Sion standeth very firmly stedfast,
Never once shaking: soe, on high, Jehova
Who his hope buildeth, very firmly stedfast,
      Ever abideth.
        [Mary Sidney, "Psalm 125 Qui Confidunt," ca. 1590]

So the goddess fled from her place, with awful
Sound of feet and thunder of wings around her
While behind a clamour of winging women
      Severed the twilight.
        [Algernon Charles Swinburne, "Sapphics," 1884]

Ottava rima p. 17

That day and night she wandred here and there,
And halfe the other day that did ensue
Untill at last she was arrived where
A fine young grove with pleasant shadow grew
Near to the which two litle rivers were
Whose moisture did the tender herbs renue
And make a sweete and very pleasing sound
By running on the sand and stonie ground.
        [Ludovico Ariosto, Orlando Furioso I, 35,
          translated by Sir John Harington, 1591]

Perfect she was, but as perfection is
   Insipid in this naughty world of ours,
Where our first parents never learned to kiss
   Till they were exiled from their earlier bowers,
Where all was peace, and innocence, and bliss
   (I wonder how they got through the twelve hours)

Don José, like a lineal son of Eve,
Went plucking various fruit without her leave.
                              [Lord Byron, Don Juan I, *xviii, 1818]*

The same rhyme-pattern in tetrameter

Nigh seated where the river flowes
    That watreth Babells thanckfull plaine,
Which then our teares in pearled rowes
    Did help to water with their raine,
The thought of Sion bred such woes,
    That though our harpes we did retaine,
Yet uselesse, and untouched there
On willowes only hanged they were.
              [Mary Sidney, "Psalm 137: Super Flumina," *ca. 1590]*

Rhyme royal p. 18

A thousand lamentable objects there,
In scorn of nature, art gave lifeless life:
Many a dry drop seem'd a weeping tear,
Shed for the slaughter'd husband by the wife;
The red blood reek'd to show the painter's strife,
    And dying eyes gleam'd forth their ashy lights,
    Like dying coals burnt out in tedious nights.
                        [William Shakespeare, Lucrece, *1594]*

Spenserian stanza p. 18

    The joyous birdes, shrouded in chearefull shade,
    Their notes unto the voice attempred sweet:
    Th'angelicall soft tremblyng voyces made
    To th'instruments divine respondence meet:
    The silver-sounding instruments did meete
    In the base murmure of the waters fall.
    The waters fall, with difference discreet,
    Now soft, no loud, unto the wind did call:
The gentle warbling wind low answered to all.
                [Edmund Spenser, The Faerie Queene II, 12.71, *1590]*

Each sound, too, here to languishment inclin'd
Lull'd the weak bosom, and inducèd ease
Aerial music in the warbling wind,
At distance rising oft, by small degrees
Nearer and nearer came, till o'er the trees
It hung, and breath'd such soul-dissolving airs,
As did, alas! with soft perdition please:
Entangled deep in its enchanting snares,
The listening heart forgot all duties and all cares.
                [*James Thomson,* The Castle of Indolence *I, 1748*]

Roll on, thou deep and dark blue Ocean—roll!
Ten thousand fleets sweep over thee in vain;
Man marks the earth with ruin—his control
Stops with the shore;—upon the watery plain
The wrecks are all thy deed, nor doth remain
A shadow of man's ravage, save his own,
When for a moment, like a drop of rain,
He sinks into thy depths with bubbling groan,
Without a grave, unknelled uncoffined and unknown.
                [*Lord Byron,* Childe Harold's Pilgrimage *IV, 1812*]

SYLLABIC METERS pp. 23–24

Lines of twelve

Perch'd on the upland wheatfields beyond the village end
a red-brick Windmill stood with black bonnet of wood
that trimm'd the whirling cross of its great arms around
upon the wind, pumping up water night and day
from the deep Kentish chalk to feed a little town
where miniatured afar it huddled on the coast
its glistening roofs and thrust its short pier in the sea.
                [*Robert Bridges, "Kate's Mother," 1921*]

Stanza of seven, ten, six, six, eight, twelve, six

    Although the aepyornis

or roc that lived in Madagascar, and
the moa are extinct,
the camel-sparrow, linked
    with them in size—the large sparrow
Xenophon saw walking by a stream—was and is
a symbol of justice.
> [Marianne Moore, "He 'Digesteth Hard Yron,'" 1941]

Stanza of eleven, eleven, nine, ten

When there are so many we shall have to mourn,
when grief has been made so public, and exposed
        to the critique of a whole epoch
the frailty of our conscience and anguish,
> [W. H. Auden, "In Memory of Sigmund Freud," 1939]

Stanza of eight, six, eight, six, eight, six, eight, six, eight, ten

Late in the afternoon the light
        at this tapering end
Of Long Island not so much fails
        as filters out the sun,
and in a month amid stances
        restores the word twilight
to its original senses:
        the day between, or half
itself, as when Locke alluded
        to "the twilight of probability"
> [Richard Howard, "Crepuscular," 1967]

Haiku pp. 24–25

Evening star so soon?
No. Low in the March sunset
Turning, a jet lands.
> [John Hollander, "A Bright Light Shines in the West," 1975]

Cinquain p. 25

Just now,
Out of the strange
Still dusk . . . as strange, as still . .

A white moth flew. Why am I grown
So cold?

[Adelaide Crapsey, "The Warning," 1913]

TERZA RIMA p. 18

The thief, when he had done with prophecy,
     made figs of both his lifted hands, and cried
     "Take these, O God, for they are aimed at Thee!"

Then was my heart upon the serpents' side,
     for 'round his neck one coiled like a garotte
     as if to say, "Enough of ranting pride,"

And another pinned his arms, and tied a knot
     of head and tail in front of him again,
     so tightly that they could not stir one jot.

[Dante Alighieri, Inferno XXV,
translated by Richard Wilbur, 1993]

As in that trance of wondrous thought I lay
     This was the tenor of my waking dream.
Methought I sate beside a public way

     Thick strewn with summer dust, and a great stream
Of people there was hurrying to and fro
     Numerous as gnats upon the evening gleam,

All hastening onward, yet none seemed to know
     Wither he went, or whence he came, and I
He made one of the multitude, yet so

     Was borne amid the crowd as through the sky
One of the million leaves of summer's bier.—
     Old age and youth, manhood and infancy,

Mixed in one mighty torrent did appear,
     Some flying from the thing they feared, and some
Seeking the object of another's fear . . .

[Percy Bysshe Shelley, The Triumph of Life, *1824]*

TRIOLET p. 43

Since mistletoe is hard to find,
    We do not need it, Mollie.
Oh! do I beg of you be kind;
Since mistletoe is hard to find,
Pretend that you are color-blind
    And kiss beneath the holly.
Since mistletoe is hard to find,
    We do not need it, Mollie.
                    [Thomas Augustine Daly, "Mistletoe and Holly," 1906]

TRIOLET ADAPTED

We'll walk the woods no more,
But stay beside the fire,
To weep for old desire
And things that are no more.
    The woods are spoiled and hoar,
The ways are full of mire;
We'll walk the woods no more,
But stay beside the fire.
    We loved, in days of yore,
Love, laughter, and the lyre.
Ah God, but death is dire,
And death is at the door—
We'll walk the woods no more.
        [Robert Louis Stevenson, "Nous n'irons plus au bois," 1875]

TROCHEES IN TETRAMETER p. 8

Reason, in itself confounded,
Saw division grow together
                [William Shakespeare, "The Phoenix and Turtle," 1601]

VERBAL MIMESIS pp. 51–54

Some semantic effects

. . . And then there crept

A little noiseless noise among the leaves
Born of the very *sigh* that *silence* heaves
> [*John Keats, "I Stood Tip-toe," 1817*]

And *sigh* the lack of many a thing I *sought*
> [*William Shakespeare, Sonnet 30, 1609*]

Patience hardens to a pittance, courage
unflinchingly declines into sour rage,
the cobweb-banners, the shrill bugle-bands
and the bronze warriors resting on their wounds.
> [*Geoffrey Hill, "The Mystery of the
> Charity of Charles Péguy," 1984*]

Between one floating realm unseen powers rule
(Rod upon mild silver rod, like meter
Broken in fleet cahoots with subject matter)
And one we feel is ours, and call the real, . . .
> [*James Merrill, "The Book of Ephraim: Section 'F'," 1976*]

Some syntactic effects

[1]
In the afternoon they came unto a land
In which it seemèd always afternoon.
All round the coast the languid air did swoon,
Breathing like one that hath a weary dream.
Full-faced above the valley stood the moon;
And like a downward smoke, the slender stream
Along the cliff to fall and pause and fall did seem.
> [*Lord Alfred Tennyson, "The Lotos-Eaters," 1832*]

[2a]
Then in the blazon of sweet beauty's best—
Of hand, of foot, of lip, of eye, of brow—
I see their antique pen would have expressed
Even such a beauty as you master now.
> [*William Shakespeare, Sonnet 106, 1609*]

[2b]
O'er many a frozen, many a fiery alp,

Rocks, caves, lakes, fens, bogs, dens, and shades of
    death,
A universe of death, which God by curse
Created evil, for evil only good . . .
                              [*John Milton*, Paradise Lost *II, 1674*]

[3]
Their song was partial, but the harmony
(What could it less when spirits immortal sing?)
Suspended hell, and took with ravishment
The thronging audience. In discourse more sweet
(For eloquence the soul, song charms the sense)
                              [*John Milton*, Paradise Lost *II, 1674*)

[4]
    But what you in compassion ought
    Shall now in my revenge be wrought;
    And flowers, and grass, and I and all,
    Will in one common ruin fall.
    For Juliana comes, and she
What I do to the grass, does to my thoughts and me.
                        [*Andrew Marvell*, "The Mower's Song," *1681*]

[5]
                        and these eyes will find
The men I knew, and watch the chariot whirl
About the goal again, and hunters race
The shadowy lion, and the warrior-kings,
In height and prowess more than human, strive
Again for glory, while the golden lyre
Is ever sounding in heroic ears
Heroic hymns, and every way the vales
Wind, clouded with the grateful incense-fume
Of those who mix all odour to the Gods
On one far height, in one far-shining fire.
                        [*Lord Alfred Tennyson*, "Tiresias," *1885*]

Some rhythmic effects

And Job, I must have him there past mistake,
The man of Uz (and Us without the z,
Painters who need his patience). Well, all these,

Secure in their devotion, up shall come
Out of a corner when you least expect,
As one by a dark stair into a great light,
Music and talking . . .

> *[Robert Browning, "Fra Lippo Lippi," 1888]*

Aye, on the shores of darkness there is light,
 And precipices show untrodden green;
There is a budding morrow in midnight,
 There is a triple sight in blindness keen . . .

> *[John Keats, "To Homer," 1818]*

I'll walk where my own nature would be leading—
 It vexes me to choose another guide—
Where the grey flocks in ferny glens are feeding,
 Where the wild wind blows on the mountainside . . .

> *[Emily Brontë, "Stanzas," 1850]*

          He always kept his poise
To the top branches, climbing carefully
With the same pains you use to fill a cup
Up to the brim, and even above the brim.
Then he flung outward, feet first, with a swish,
Kicking his way down through the air to the ground.

> *[Robert Frost, "Birches," 1916]*

VILLANELLE p. 40

In the clatter of a train
 Is a promise brisk and bright.
I shall see my love again!

I am tired and fagged and fain;
 But I feel a still delight
In the clatter of the train,

Hurry-hurrying on amain
 Through the moonshine thin and white—
I shall see my love again!

Many noisy miles remain;
   But a sympathetic sprite
In the clatter of the train

Hammers cheerful:—that the strain
   Once concluded and the fight
I shall see my love again.

Yes, the overword is plain,—
   If it's trivial, if it's trite—
In the clatter of the train:
"I shall see my love again."
              [William Ernest Henley, "Villanelle," 1897]

ZEUGMA p. 48

Or stain her honor, or her new brocade . . .

Or lose her heart, or necklace, at a ball . . .
              [Alexander Pope, The Rape of the Lock, *1714]*

SUGGESTIONS FOR FURTHER READING

Paul Fussell's *Poetic Meter and Poetic Form* (rev. ed., New York, 1979) is an excellent discursive introduction to some of the problems of prosodic analysis. The essays in Harvey Gross, ed., *The Structure of Verse: Modern Essays on Prosody* (rev. ed., New York, 1979) cover an array of problems and views. My own *Vision and Resonance* (2d. ed., New Haven, 1985) includes discussions of formal problems of a more specialized nature, and in *Melodious Guile* (New Haven, 1988) I explore some of the complex relations between scheme and trope in poetic practice which are hinted at on pp. 52–54, above. Two brilliant essays of the late W. K. Wimsatt underlie most contemporary discussions: "One Relation of Rhyme to Reason," in *The Verbal Icon* (Lexington, Ky., 1954) and "In Search of Verbal Mimesis," in *The Day of the Leopards* (New Haven, 1976). Wimsatt also edited a most valuable handbook of comparative metrics called *Versification: Major Language Types* (New York, 1972); pp. 191–252 are devoted to English prosody and its problems. Individual entries in the *Princeton Encyclopedia of Poetry and Poetics* (enlarged ed., Princeton, 1974) of metrical interest include larger discussions such as "Meter," "Prosody," "Verse and Prose," "Music and Poetry," "Song," "Concrete Poetry," etc., as well as essays on many national literatures, East and West. In addition there is a multitude of smaller notes on particular forms, prosodic terms, etc. A useful selection from this comprehensive volume, with new entries and updated versions of previous ones, has also been published as *The Princeton Handbook of Poetic Terms*. It can be warmly recommended to general and advanced readers. George Saintsbury's *A History of English Prosody from the Twelfth Century to the Present Day* is exhaustive and slow-paced; the portion of it reprinted as *Historical Manual of*

English Prosody will probably be more useful to all but a handful of specialists.

A brilliant analysis of prosody, meter, and rhythm in its various uses in English verse is to be found in Derek Attridge's *The Rhythms of English Poetry* (London and New York, 1982). More limited in scope and subject are such studies as those of Attridge on quantitative verse in English—*Well-Weigh'd Syllables* (Cambridge, 1976)—or Helen Louise Cohen, *Lyric Forms from France* (New York, 1922). Harvey Gross, *Sound and Form in Modern Poetry* (Ann Arbor, 1964), and John Thompson, *The Founding of English Metre* (2d. ed., New York, 1988), shed reasonable light on obscure questions. Robert Bridges, *Milton's Prosody* (Oxford, 1921), and Edward M. Weismiller, "Studies of Verse Form in the Minor English Poems," in *A Variorum Commentary on the Poems of John Milton* II, pt. 3 (New York, 1972), both raise important general questions. Donald Wesling, *The Chances of Rhyme: Device and Modernity* (Berkeley and Los Angeles, 1980), is brief and provocative; T. S. Omond, *English Metrists*, is an ultimately amusing account of the contentions and pedantries of prosodic theorists in English. Catherine Ing, in *Elizabethan Lyrics* (London, 1951), pays some illuminating attention to the relations between verse and musical structures, and Elise B. Jorgens, *The Well-Tun'd Word* (Minneapolis, 1981), examines in detail the transformation of verse into song in the seventeenth century. George Puttenham's *The Arte of English Poesie* (1589) is still of great interest for both prosody and rhetoric, the latter of which is cleverly and usefully served by Richard A. Lanham, *A Handbook of Rhetorical Terms* (Berkeley and Los Angeles, 1969). For transcendent afterthoughts on many of these matters, Justus George Lawler's *Celestial Pantomime* (New Haven, 1979) is remarkable, but cannot be recommended to beginners. Some of the great Roman Jakobson's essays of most interest for readers of poetry in English have been selected and annotated in a volume called *Language and Literature* (Cambridge, Mass., 1987). A truly monumental guide through all that was written on various aspects of the nature and structure of English verse is that of T. V. F. Brogan, *English Versification, 1570–1980* (Baltimore, 1981). It is at once a comprehensive bibliography and a masterful analytic classification in its own right, and the annotations and abstracts will be of the greatest value to all students of poetry. Finally, Barbara Herrnstein Smith's *Poetic Closure: A Study of the Way Poems End* (Chicago, 1968) remains cogent and useful.

INDEX